D1029327

THE IMPOSSIBLE JOURNEY
OF SIR ERNEST SHACKLETON

SOUTH AMERICA

Falkland Islands

SOUTH GEORGIA

Elephant Island
Joinville Island
Paulet Island

WEDDELL SEA

SOUTH POLE

THE IMPOSSIBLE Journey of SIR ERNEST Shackleton

BY

WILLIAM BIXBY

J 919.9 B

4717

AN ATLANTIC MONTHLY PRESS BOOK

BOSTON · LITTLE, BROWN AND COMPANY · TORONTO

COPYRIGHT, ©, 1960, BY WILLIAM BIXBY

LIBRARY OF CONGRESS CATALOG CARD NO. 60-5871

THIRD PRINTING

ATLANTIC—LITTLE, BROWN BOOKS
ARE PUBLISHED BY
LITTLE, BROWN AND COMPANY
IN ASSOCIATION WITH
THE ATLANTIC MONTHLY PRESS

Published simultaneously in Canada
by Little, Brown & Company (Canada) Limited

PRINTED IN THE UNITED STATES OF AMERICA

CONTENTS

	Members of the Weddell Sea Party	vii
	Prologue	3
1	Southward	8
2	Ice	18
3	Catastrophe	33
4	On the Pack Ice	40
5	Patience	62
6	Escape	80
7	The Freezing Sea	92
8	The Inhospitable Island	116
9	The One Chance Taken	136
10	Those Left Behind	154
11	Storm-Wracked	163
12	Too-Solid Land	173
13	Beyond Endurance	181
14	Strange Welcome	201
	Epilogue	204

MEMBERS OF THE WEDDELL SEA PARTY

Imperial Trans-Antarctic Expedition, 1914 to 1916

SIR ERNEST SHACKLETON	Expedition Leader
FRANK WILD	Second-in-Command
FRANK WORSLEY	Captain of the *Endurance*
LIONEL GREENSTREET	First Officer
THOMAS CREAN	Second Officer
ALFRED B. CHEETHAM	Third Officer
HUBERT HUDSON	Navigator
LOUIS RICKINSON	First Engineer
A. J. KERR	Second Engineer
ALEXANDER MACKLIN	Surgeon
JAMES MCILROY	Surgeon
JAMES WORDIE	Geologist
LEONARD HUSSEY	Meteorologist
REGINALD JAMES	Physicist

ROBERT CLARK	Biologist
J. F. HURLEY	Photographer
GEORGE MARSTON	Artist
THOMAS ORDE-LEES	Motor Expert
W. MCNEISH	Carpenter
CHARLES GREEN	Cook
WILLIAM BAKEWELL	Able Seaman
WALTER HOW	Able Seaman
TIMOTHY MCCARTHY	Able Seaman
JOHN VINCENT	Able Seaman
A. HOLNESS	Fireman
THOMAS MCLEOD	Fireman
WILLIAM STEVENSON	Fireman
PERCE BLACKBORO	Steward (originally stowed away)

THE IMPOSSIBLE JOURNEY
OF SIR ERNEST SHACKLETON

PROLOGUE

Polar exploration is at once the cleanest and most isolated way of having a bad time which has been devised.

> The Worst Journey in the World
> by APSLEY CHERRY-GARRARD

DURING the Antarctic summer of 1957-1958 a British Commonwealth expedition led by Sir Vivian Fuchs completed the first crossing of the Antarctic continent from sea to sea. The journey covered 2158 miles and took ninety-nine days. National honor came to the Commonwealth and personal honor to the men who made the crossing. New land was explored — for the eastern side of the continent between the South Pole and the Weddell Sea had never been traveled before. In addition, mapping, geological prospecting, seismological work and meteorological observations added quantities of scientific information to man's increasing knowledge of the earth.

The same goals won by Fuchs were sought and lost more than forty years ago by an Antarctic pioneer: Sir Ernest Shackleton. The odds against crossing the continent in the technologically primitive era of 1914 were staggering. Shackleton had no airplane, no reliable radio, no radar, no snow tractors, no neighboring bases or ships from which rescue could come. All he had was a wooden ship, sledges, sledge dogs and what has been described in deprecatory tones as a motley crew. He and the expedition also were deeply in debt when the attempt was made. Despite all this, Shackleton was eager for the scientific knowledge to be gained and the glory to be won.

England had need of glory at that moment. Two years before Shackleton sailed, Captain Scott and his polar party had been beaten in the race to the South Pole by Norway's veteran explorer, Roald Amundsen. To make the matter tragic as well as humiliating, Scott and all his companions died on their way back from the Pole.

To recover lost prestige for his country was one of Shackleton's aims. To gain scientific knowledge was another. Still a third was the accomplishment of the last great adventure left to polar exploration: the transcontinental crossing. The original scheme was not Shackleton's. In 1908, Dr. William S. Bruce, a noted explorer in his own right, conceived the idea. But he deferred to Shackleton who could gain popular support — meaning money — for the expedition.

When Shackleton set sail from England in August, 1914, at the outset of World War I, he was heading to the Antarctic for the third time. He had served with Scott in 1901; he had led his own expedition to within a hundred miles of the Pole in 1909. And he had found that whatever else he tried to do or be, he was best fitted to lead polar expeditions.

The late Sir Hubert Wilkins has described Shackleton as the greatest of all British polar explorers. Comparing polar explorers is dangerous business. But one of Scott's men, Apsley Cherry-Garrard, has written: "For a joint scientific and geographical piece of organization, give me Scott; for a winter journey, Wilson; for a dash to the pole and nothing else, Amundsen; and if I am in a devil of a hole and want to get out of it, give me Shackleton every time."

The personal goals of these leaders and the men they commanded differed widely. Some went to the Antarctic for purely scientific purposes; some to gain glory for their countries and, not at all incidentally, for themselves; others went solely because of a love of adventure — and some went for all three reasons.

Superficially there appear to be few differences among the men who go South. In their courage they do not differ. There are those who go resolved to endure separation from society, emotional starvation, the pain of cold and frostbite, the depressing effects of the long Antarctic night. But they dream of returning home.

Another type of man goes South with no regret at leaving the everyday world of men. He goes eagerly and with no backward glance and finds, in the snow-filled desolation of the polar regions, a larger vision of existence that alone gives meaning to his life. He goes because he loves it. He is happier in a hut on the frozen shores of a frozen sea than he ever could be in shop, bank or office.

To such men modern civilized life is suffocating,

meaningless, deadening. They can be found in mining camps in the North, at the outermost limits of human settlements, on the shores of South Georgia Island where they run the whaling stations. They are to be found in isolated mountainous or desert places — and on the decks of tramp steamers on all the oceans of the world.

They are the misfits of the world. Most of them, unfortunately, have neither the talent nor the training to let them remain physically in a humdrum world while they escape mentally into art or science or philosophy like Picasso, Newton and Spinoza.

"Exploration," it has been well said, "is the physical expression of the intellectual passion." And many misfits have taken that path to find a meaningful life.

Shackleton was such a man. And it is to him, and to all men of his stamp, that this book is respectfully dedicated.

W. B.

one
SOUTHWARD

ELEVEN hundred miles east of Cape Horn in the South Atlantic Ocean lies the small, mountainous, snow-covered island of South Georgia. It is called the gateway to the Antarctic. Ships going down into the ice from Atlantic ports pause here for final loading of supplies, for a last look at the world of men. On December 4, 1914, on the island's eastern tip in a small indentation of Stromness Bay called Grytviken Harbor, lay several ships. All but one were whalers. That one was a small 350-ton barkentine named the *Endurance*. She was powered by both sail and steam. Her sleek wooden hull was especially reinforced to withstand ice pressure. Heavily laden, she lay low in the water. To old whalemen on shore, the *Endurance* presented a familiar scene: another expedition on its way south.

The only permanent inhabitants of South Georgia are whalemen and workers in the whale factories. Whaleships return at the end of the hunting season to discharge their catch and tie up for the long winter months. The stations, operated by Norwegians and Britons, huddle on the easternmost shore of the island to escape hurricanes that sweep all the way from Cape Horn across the subantarctic seas and fall with paralyzing fury on the small jut of ice and rock that is South Georgia.

The stations line Stromness Bay. Behind them rise sheer cliffs of rock and ice. No one has tried to penetrate the interior of South Georgia. Only the eyes of gulls and wandering albatrosses look down occasionally on the icy wasteland behind the mountains.

Small boats moved back and forth from the side of the *Endurance* to the shore. The mound of coal bags at the quayside became smaller with each trip. Winches aboard the ship whined and clattered. Unharmonious howls from the throats of seventy halfwild Canadian sledge dogs greeted the arrival and hoisting aboard of great slabs of whalemeat — the dogs' ration for the days ahead. A ton of unsightly meat was hauled aloft and secured to the spars and rigging of the masts, out of reach, if not out of mind, of the dogs.

As the coal bags came aboard, they were stacked and lashed securely on deck. There was no room below. Bunkers were full and every inch of space packed tight with sledges, rations, clothing, tents, sleeping bags — all the equipment that two years of planning had produced. There could be no turning back for forgotten items. One overlooked necessity could cause months of discomfort, the death of a man, or wreck the entire expedition.

When one of the boats unloaded at the ship's side, a man detached himself from the group on the bridge and scrambled nimbly overside into the small craft. Oarsmen pulled rhythmically across the quiet waters of the harbor to shore. The man jumped out before the bow of the boat grated on the rocks and he hurried up the beach toward the station manager's office. He walked leaning forward slightly as though pushing against some invisible obstacle. His shoulders were hunched, his head thrust forward. He was of no more than medium height yet he gave the impression of great size. He had big shoulders, a bullneck and a square jaw. As he walked his alert eyes scanned the dwindling pile of supplies. As he approached the door to the office in the hut back from the shore, he shifted the roll of charts to his other hand and knocked briskly on the worn panel.

When the door was opened, the frown of concentration left his face and was replaced by a wide, disarming grin. He shook hands with his old friend Mr. Sorlle, the station manager. Together the two men went to a table around which several bearded whaling captains were seated.

They all greeted the man who had entered with gruff good humor and familiarity. Sir Ernest Shackleton was no stranger among them. This was his third venture into the ice, into the Antarctic.

Charts were unrolled and the talk began. The calloused forefinger of a huge Norwegian whaler pointed toward the South Sandwich Island group. The man spoke quickly — in Norwegian. Mr. Sorlle translated. The words brought a frown to Shackleton's face again.

Even in the summer, now at its height in those latitudes, ice often closed the northern edge of the Weddell Sea to whalers. The whalemen shook their heads pessimistically. This year whaleships had encountered heavy pack ice farther north than ever before. The outlook was not favorable.

Shackleton instantly absorbed the bad news. As the men talked, his eyes scanned the charts. His glance traveled east above the South Sandwich group, then south into the Weddell Sea to the little-known shores of the Antarctic continent itself. Ice lay between him and his goal, thousands upon thousands of square miles of thick, heaving, grinding ice. But there was no turning back to England or South America. The expedition had to go on now or give up — ice or no ice.

The whalemen fell silent.

Shackleton spoke. As he talked, his finger traced a course. His hand scooped down into the Weddell Sea from its eastern edge, down farther south to its most southerly point. The tips of his curled fingers came to rest on the western shores of the sea and he tapped that part of the chart for emphasis.

The ice, he was saying, moved in a great semi-circle, clockwise, drifting much as the ice pack in the Arctic Sea moved. If he entered from the east he could work his way down and — with luck — make a landing where he could establish a base. The greatest danger area was to the west against the rocky coast of Graham Land (Palmer Peninsula), where ice jammed against the land and incalculable pressure developed that extended as much as two hundred miles out into the sea.

Several of the whalemen murmured hesitantly. Most remained silent. Shackleton rolled up the charts and solemnly shook hands with the Norwegians. They returned his grip with warmth and good wishes but it was obvious that they felt his venture was a bad risk.

Shackleton's jaw was set stubbornly as he left the meeting. He couldn't turn back. Not now. Not with what lay behind him. Four months before, on the eve of his departure from England, war had been declared. On that critical day in August, 1914, the *Endurance* lay off the English coast ready to head South. Years of preparations and plans were complete; thousands of pounds had been spent. But Shackleton offered to cancel the expedition and release himself and his men for war service.

The initial reply to his proposal was brief and to the point. A cable arrived, bearing a one-word message: PROCEED. It was signed by Winston Churchill, First Lord of the Admiralty.

Now, walking toward the shore with Mr. Sorlle, Shackleton knew he had to proceed, with or without the help of Nature.

On board the *Endurance* once more, Shackleton returned to the bridge. The sun was lowering in the sky and the wind from the glittering peaks behind Stromness was cold. Wisps of clouds came over the mountains. Shackleton conferred with his second-in-command, a man as different in appearance from Shackleton as could be imagined. Frank Wild was slim, wiry, red-haired and blue-eyed. As he lounged comfortably on the bridge, he viewed the hubbub on the decks with detachment and smoked his pipe.

When Shackleton told him of the ice problem, Wild listened, nodding from time to time. He showed no concern.

"We'll leave in the morning," Shackleton said, his jaw pushed out pugnaciously. He turned to the third man on the bridge, the ship's captain, Frank Worsley. "What's the weather going to be, Skipper?"

Worsley looked at the sky and at the oncoming clouds. "It'll probably snow a little. But otherwise fine."

Unlike Shackleton and Wild, Worsley was new to the Antarctic — but not to adventure. He had sailed tropical seas for pearls and struggled with northern ice off Newfoundland. Physically he resembled Shackleton. He had a short, powerful body, square-jawed face. A hint of recklessness perpetually gleamed in his eyes.

Shackleton left the bridge again, this time to make a final check on the stowing of cargo. All coal was aboard; the last lines were secured. The dogs continued to snarl and snap at each other and at passers-by from their kennels on deck.

As he moved among the men — scientists, sailors, engineers and ship's officers — Shackleton told them of the departure time. No detail of the men's work escaped his quick glance — and shoddy stowage brought sharp reprimand. The men hastily corrected mistakes, checking and rechecking their gear.

Altogether there were twenty-eight men aboard the *Endurance*. Seven had had Antarctic experience; the remainder had none. When they had been signed, Shackleton had told them plainly of the work ahead. Scientists would work alongside able-bodied seamen. Everyone, from the expedition's artist to the two doctors would pitch in wherever needed.

Economizing had cut the party to so small a group that no one member could reserve his efforts for his specialty alone — whether it was geology or rope splicing. Everyone had fallen to, clearing decks and making everything secure. The scientists, all thumbs when it came to tying knots or responding to shipboard commands, grinned and took the expected chaffing from experienced seamen.

When darkness fell, all hands except a skeleton watch went ashore to a farewell party. There was little gaiety. Mr. Sorlle and the whalemen wished the departing men good luck. It was a heartfelt wish. They knew the expedition needed all the luck it could get. Many of the whalemen had attended similar parties and had shaken hands with men who had gone into the ice and not returned.

That night the dogs whimpered and howled. The men slept fitfully in their bunks. Those who had been South before were restless with anticipation; those who had not speculated on what lay ahead. The dark hours passed.

The morning of December 5, 1914, was gray and overcast on South Georgia. At 8:30 orders came from the bridge to weigh anchor. The windlass clattered and the anchor chain clanked through the hawsepipe. Whalemen on shore waved a final good-by, and amid squalls of snow and sleet the bow of the *Endurance* turned South.

two
ICE

THE plan of Shackleton's expedition was as bold as it was ambitious. Fourteen men of the Weddell Sea party aboard the *Endurance* were to establish a base on the Antarctic continent. Six would head for the Pole and beyond to the Ross Sea side of the continent, a distance of about two thousand miles. A support party from the expedition's other ship, *Aurora,* was to meet them on the Beardmore glacier. A party of three would go east from the Weddell Sea camp and explore Enderby Land — a vast stretch of unknown territory. Still another three-man party would proceed west toward Graham Land. All would make geological and meteorological observations as well as gather geographic data. Two men of the shore party were to remain at the base. Those left aboard the *Endurance* were to sail to Graham Land and trace the as yet uncharted coastline there.

But first the ice had to be conquered.

On the morning of the third day after leaving South Georgia, the lookout called down and pointed to the horizon. For a long moment the officers on the bridge squinted across the swelling sea. Shackleton grabbed Worsley's arm in excitement. Then Worsley himself saw it: the long, low line of pack ice stretching away to a thread on the horizon.

The men crowded the railing and were silent. For many it was a first encounter. Even veterans of the Antarctic were quiet. The greenest man knew without being told that ice was the first big obstacle to be overcome.

For days the *Endurance* coasted the pack as Worsley and Shackleton looked for leads or lanes of open water through which the ship could pass. The pack in this latitude was loose and for a while the *Endurance* made good progress. But as she moved farther south, the pack became closer and then the work began for which the ship had been designed. When the ship was surrounded by thick ice floes, Worsley would order full speed ahead and the ship would ram a floe once, twice or three times with its reinforced, knifelike prow to split open the ice. When his efforts paid off, the ship would move ahead to the next floe and there begin all over again.

Shackleton watched from the bridge, keeping an eye on the weather and the state of the ice. The air became colder; snow squalls struck more frequently. On many days the sky was overcast and then Worsley could navigate the ship using the "ice blink." This helpful trick of nature gave a navigator a more far-reaching picture of the sea and ice ahead than his own eyesight. Light reflected from areas of ice showed up white on the underside of the cloud cover. Open water showed black. Leads between floes appeared as dark lines that could be followed to areas of open sea. By taking advantage of this natural radar screen, Worsley confidently worked the ship southward.

On clear days, when the sun sparkled on the sea and the great icebergs were so dazzling that they blinded an onlooker, Worsley had to slow down and search for leads or make his own in the pack. Navigating became more difficult. Even on such clear days Worsley spent hours waiting to get a sun "fix" with his sextant. Although the sun was visible, the horizon was distorted by mirages — and a navigator must have a stable and true horizon. The mirages came from the refraction of light through areas of cold air over the ice and warmer air over the open water. Icebergs and hummocks appeared drawn up and misshapen. The tops of bergs boiled up into the sky assuming fantastic shapes. The strange distortions appeared as towers and cathedrals, or as block upon block of sunlit houses. At times Worsley, squinting through the eyepiece, thought he was looking at an entire city. Then in an instant the weird shapes would vanish or re-form into other patterns equally fantastic or slowly dissolve into smudges which trailed away into nothingness across the strange sky.

Shackleton spent more and more time on the bridge. He paced back and forth, shoulders hunched forward, his eyes always on the horizon. On the thirty-fifth day out of South Georgia he saw what he was looking for: the Antarctic continent. He called Wild to the bridge and, pipe alight, Wild came up and stood beside him. Together they looked across the ice at the line of coast in the distance. At the sight of land the usually imperturbable

Wild became excited. Puffs of smoke came faster from his pipe and his blue eyes shone with anticipation.

Soon the *Endurance* was skirting that part of the continent called Coats Land. A few days later uncharted land was sighted and mapped. Shackleton named the newly discovered shore Caird Coast in honor of his biggest backer at home. For a brief time they stopped in a small bight which Shackleton named Glacier Bay. Then the *Endurance* moved west and south, deeper into the Weddell Sea toward the proposed landing place near Vahsel Bay. All the way the ship battled the ice. The sun hung above the horizon around the clock. There was no night for it was Antarctic summer. Darkness came only when blizzards howled down on the ship and heavy clouds obscured the sun. As the ship worked along the coast, Worsley held as close to the continent's edge as possible for it offered shelter and some open water. But from time to time they had to move out into the pack ice to get around icebergs which were stranded on the shoaling sea floor.

The ship would work into the wind-driven ice, nose around the berg and head back for the shelter of the coast. At these times Shackleton worried. He knew what would happen if a storm should spring up as the ship was edging around a berg and he always sighed with relief when the ship was once more safely inshore.

Then one day it happened. The *Endurance* had to go out into the ice. The sky darkened. A driving east-northeast wind sprang up. Ice, driven by the gale, closed around the ship, cutting off the route back toward shore. The temperature dropped suddenly as wind drove the pack against the ship closing all navigable leads. The ice itself crumpled under the pressure of more distant moving floes. Corrugations appeared in the ice surface; hummocks rose across the pack. Worsley ordered full steam and the ship struggled to break free. Shackleton watched, listened and hoped, waiting for a shift in the wind or a slackening of the storm. But for days the gale continued. When it finally blew itself out the *Endurance* was caught fast. That day was January 18, 1915.

As hope of freeing the ship faded, Shackleton, with Wild and Worsley, planned the long wait through the approaching Antarctic winter until another spring when the pack would loosen its grip. Worsley, new to the ice, relied on Shackleton and Wild for information. They both assured him that, with patience, they'd be on their way in the spring. Yet already in Shackleton's mind there was the foreboding that they might never be set free.

Soon after the ship was frozen in, Shackleton ordered the fires put out to save coal. Scientists and officers bunked in deck housings greeted his next order with enthusiasm. McNeish, the ship's carpenter, was set to work converting the now nearly empty forehold into below-deck quarters where the men could keep warm and where they would have a snug bunk away from the whistling wind and the seeping cold. When it was done, the men moved in, dragging their personal gear down from the windswept deck. Though small, their new quarters were so much warmer than their former ones that they promptly named it the Ritz. The space had been divided into a common area with bunk cubicles around the sides. Each "cabin" had two or four bunks in it. The men chose bunkmates and began decorating and naming their cubicles. The engineers had no chance to name theirs — it was promptly dubbed "The Nuts." The remaining cabins became "The Billabong," "The Sailor's Rest," "The Fumarole," "The Anchorage," and, most appropriate of all, "Auld Reekie."

The temperature outside the ship dropped. Sudden storms sprang up. At one moment the sun shone on the white world and the next clouds boiled up, the sky darkened and a hundred-mile-an-hour blizzard would strike the ship. The days shortened. Temperatures set new low records: 30, 40, 50 degrees below zero Fahrenheit. Snow drifted on the decks and the men worked constantly to shovel it over the side. As they labored, more snow fell, stinging the men's faces, piling higher on the ship. Ice coated the rigging and had to be chopped at with axes — and no sooner was it cleared than more formed. The pack creaked and groaned as wind drove it from hundreds of miles away against the ship. The sun disappeared to rise no more above the horizon. The long, long night began.

Thwarted once again by the force of the Antarctic, Shackleton went among his men with patience and a smile. He lounged and talked and joked with them all. He had a special joke with the youngest crew member, Perce Blackboro. The nineteen-year-old boy had stowed away on the ship when it left Buenos Aires. When he was discovered, the boy was brought to Shackleton who said angrily, "Remember, when we run out of food, you're the first one we eat." But Blackboro had pulled his weight with the men and now, grinning, Shackleton reminded him he was emergency ration number one.

To stall off boredom and depression, Shackleton kept the men on the move. They hunted seals and shot penguins and stored the frozen meat for future rations. The dogs cooped up on deck, were taken to the ice where the men built ornate "dogloos" for them. Shackleton assigned drivers who began training their teams. Soon the area around the ship became a familiar place. Lanes between hummocks and ridges were given names well known to all Englishmen. So a dog team might come racing along "Northumberland Avenue" into "Trafalgar Square" and then turn down the "Embankment" — all on Antarctic ice thousands of miles from home. The dog team drivers, new to their work, trained the half-wild animals until they formed dependable teams. Among the drivers rivalry sprang up and every night arguments filled the Ritz about which team was best. Soon all the members of the expedition became involved. Shackleton promptly announced the forthcoming Great Antarctic Dog Derby. For days preparations and more training absorbed the men.

The day for the race didn't exactly dawn. It was dark except at noon when a dim twilight filled the sky. The teams went to an opening between two ice hummocks seven hundred yards from the ship, a landmark known as the Khyber Pass, which was the starting point.

Shackleton proclaimed himself starter. He appointed Worsley judge and James, the physicist, timekeeper. The men hacked out a grandstand in the ice near the finish line and seated themselves amid an uproar of jokes, cheers and last-minute bets. Money was of no real use so the men bet their chocolate and cigarette rations. Two men at the finish line posted odds on a board slung from a crewman's neck. As an added holiday touch, the crewman wore a straw hat atop his winter headgear.

The gun cracked. The men cheered and the race was under way. The dogs strained at their harnesses and the sledges careened down the course. The men peered into the gloom trying to see which team was ahead. The barks of the dogs and shouts of the drivers grew louder as two teams came into sight. Great cheers went up from the men and a flutter of canvas handkerchiefs — to simulate a feminine element in the stands — greeted Wild's team which was the winner. Hurley, the photographer, was second. He quickly challenged Wild to another race, this time with loaded sledges.

Several days later Wild met the challenge. Each sledge, heaped with 910 pounds of ballast, started from the Khyber Pass and raced for the finish line. Wild won again. He strode about smugly smoking his pipe and looking pleased with himself. Then the judges disqualified him on the grounds that he'd lost part of his ballast near the finish line. The lost ballast was Shackleton, who had been tossed out of the sledge, roaring with laughter, when a runner hit drifted snow.

As winter storms became more frequent the men were forced to stay aboard the ship. The dogs snuggled inside their dogloos and when the snow covered the openings to their homes they poked breathing-holes through the drifted snow with their paws.

Confined to the ship, the men used all their ingenuity to keep up morale. They sang — and had a singing contest to select the worst singer of the expedition. The vote went unanimously to Shackleton.

During these monotonous weeks the ship drifted slowly with the ice pack to the north and west. The sun remained below the horizon. The expedition's only source of fresh meat disappeared as penguins and seals migrated north to open water. No living thing moved on the ice around the ship.

For many of the men the situation was not unpleasant. They were warm and safe. With all the stores, food was plentiful. They had little to do but wait for release from the ice. To while away the time the men celebrated every possible occasion. Birthdays were specialties. But the most important celebration in the Antarctic is June 22nd, Midwinter Day. In southern latitudes this day is the shortest of the year — the winter solstice. To men wrapped in Antarctic night it means the sun is on its way back above the horizon. Aboard the *Endurance,* in the Ritz, the men decorated the common room with bunting and the sledging flags. Green, the cook, prepared a feast of roast pork, gravy, stewed apples, peas, plum pudding and hot cocoa. Songs and monologues filled the evening.

The men went to bed contented. With full bellies and warm sleeping bags and a stout ship around them they slept well. There was no feeling of danger.

Alone, in his cabin aft, Shackleton lay awake, making plans. If the ice freed the ship and all went well he would return to South Georgia, refit and come back to try again. That was one possibility. About the other possibility he had not spoken to anyone. He did not have to speak of it to Wild, who had been in the Antarctic before. The two men, leader and second, were so accustomed to each other that there were little need to talk over things. But Worsley, for all his sailing and navigating skill and all his love of adventure, was still an Antarctic greenhorn — and would have to be told of the alternative.

Until late June the pack had left the *Endurance* alone. But as July approached movement and pressure in the ice began to affect her. The ship had drifted three hundred miles north, away from land, where she lay fully exposed to wind and current. On deck continuously, Shackleton watched a great ice ridge on the horizon. Day by day the ridge moved closer. The ice around the ship creaked, groaned, roared, chattered and snapped.

Standing beside the Boss one day, Worsley said, "It sounds like damned souls in torment."

Shackleton merely grunted and kept his gaze fixed on the approaching ridge. Great chunks of floe, five and more feet thick and as big as a city block, were pushed up over neighboring pieces as the pressure ridge bore down. The *Endurance* quivered as the first tremors reached the ship.

Worsley glanced at Shackleton and caught a fleeting expression of defeat on the Boss's face. It was there only an instant. Then Shackleton shook himself and hunched his shoulders. "It's a pity," he said, almost to himself. "But it can't be helped. We have to think about the men." He turned to Worsley. "Perhaps it's a pity too, Skipper, that you came to New Burlington Street in London that day we met."

Worsley shook his head. "No," he said, "I've never regretted it — and never shall, even if we don't get through."

Shackleton nodded vigorously. "Right, right," he said. He lit a cigarette and walked away.

Early the next morning while the men completed their chores, a sound like a thousand firing guns made everyone stop in his tracks. In an instant the *Endurance* was thrown over on her side until the portside lifeboats dangled only inches away from the ice.

Worsley, eating breakfast with Shackleton and Wild, was thrown against the bulkhead. Dishes flew in all directions and broke as they fell. Shouts came from all over the ship. Fearing fire from lighted stoves, Worsley crawled on all fours through the ship. He put out the fires and hurried on deck to see what was going on. The ice ridge was closer but the sudden tossing about of the ship was only a forewarning. There was more to come.

Shackleton ordered the dogs on board. A large crack appeared in the ice. In a few moments the dogloos crumpled and were buried under tons of ice. Moments later the crack in the ice disappeared as the floes came together.

Glancing up, Worsley saw the ice ridge was closer to the ship — so high it blocked the view to the northern horizon. Shackleton stood on the deckhouse giving orders. The men hurried to obey. His commands came crisp and clear above the noise of the ice. There was no confusion. Shackleton was putting into operation his other plan, his plan for disaster.

three
CATASTROPHE

IN THE loneliness of leadership, in the isolation of his cabin during the dark hours while others slept, Shackleton had planned what to do if the *Endurance* were lost. He knew now that the time of the ship's destruction was not far off.

With the hull lying on its side on the ice, he ordered sledges packed with emergency supplies put overboard and hauled to a thick floe away from the ship. He and Worsley walked around the hull and inspected the damage. Surprisingly they could see very little. But inside the *Endurance* water began to fill the holds. A few hours later the ice moved with maddening caprice, the ship righted itself and settled once more into the water. Men and sledges went back on board. All around the *Endurance* ice moved constantly. Leads opened and closed. Hummocks rose from the level white surface. The noise of breaking floes was like the continuous roar of a passing train. The men had to shout to make themselves heard.

Everyone knew now what lay ahead. None had hope that the ship could survive. Most of the men held the knowledge to themselves — there was no use discussing the inevitable. Veterans of the Antarctic like Crean and Cheetham, second and third officers, went about their work, never pausing to speculate morbidly on the situation. Greenhorns like Blackboro took the example and, save for occasional worried glances at their leader and the other officers, performed their duties briskly.

Watches were set now — four hours on, four off. To everyone it seemed that Shackleton never slept. He was present whenever a fresh watch came on and was there when it went off.

The forces of the Antarctic now seemed to mock the small ship. The weather cleared. The sun shone brilliantly. Light sparkled on the ice and flashed from the towering sides of distant bergs. The wind died until not a breath of air stirred. Yet the ice moved; the pressure grew. Sea currents far to the north were shifting the floes, pressing them against the long, curving peninsula of Graham Land to the west. Floes hummocked, jutting up suddenly and rising until breaking off. Ice rafted, sliding up over neighboring pieces and then shattering with a noise like gunshot, sending a thousand glittering splinters down onto the snow.

The pressure started beams and timbers from the frame of the ship. Side planking opened and water cascaded in. McNeish, the carpenter, quickly built a coffer dam across the lowest hold but still the water rose. Hand pumps were manned. From the deck Worsley watched water rush up from the pumps and over the side. But the stream of water pouring from the hoses slowed to a trickle and then the trickle stopped altogether.

Hurrying below, Worsley learned the pumps were frozen and fouled. He ordered gallons of boiling water to thaw them and even tried a blowtorch — but without success. He knew the pipes, if clean, were large enough to permit water to flow without freezing. But in the heaving of the ship, coal had spilled all over the lower hold. Bits of it, mixed with coal dust and bilge grease, caused the stoppage.

He looked around in the dim light. Above his head ice jammed against the ship. At any instant it might break through, letting in a cataract of black Antarctic water. Even while he stood estimating the problem the water rose above his knees. There was only one solution: move all the coal and clean the pumps fast.

Worsley sent the pump gang on deck. He went up himself and called for volunteers for the dangerous work. Two officers, Greenstreet and Hudson, stepped forward and went below with the Skipper. The water was nearly waist-high. With the air temperature only seven degrees above zero, the men plunged their arms into the cold water and began their work.

Over their heads the ice shifted and planking snapped at irregular intervals. Cold as they were, the men felt the sweat of fear on their foreheads. One more snap of a plank or crack of a timber might seal them forever in the hold below the ice. Hour after hour they picked up coal from around the pumps and threw it into bunkers. Hands and arms were numb. Backs ached. The water continued to rise. Ice formed on the surface cracking sharply when they broke through. But the pumps were cleared.

As the pump gang returned to its work, Worsley, Greenstreet and Hudson climbed out of the hold that might well have been their tomb, and drank cups of steaming cocoa. They were silent. All knew what could have happened.

The ice now seemed to be waiting. The pressure did not lessen but the air remained calm and after two days of windless weather the *Endurance* was finally pumped dry.

The respite was brief. Standing on the bridge three days later with Worsley, Shackleton pointed to an ice pressure ridge off the starboard beam. It was larger than the one that had thrown the ship on the ice. Without speaking, Shackleton turned and pointed to another ridge off the port bow — and yet another on the port quarter. All three were bearing down on the *Endurance*, moving with steady, irresistible force.

All three ridges struck the *Endurance* at the same time. From stem to stern the ship bent like a bow. Rigging whined under the stress. Timbers and beams buckled with a noise like cannon. Water again poured into the ship. The rudder and sternpost were torn away with a deafening roar. The ship lurched and shuddered like a dying animal. Sledges were lowered once more to safe floes and extra food quickly carried away from the ship. The ice ridge on the port bow began to slide up over the rail. The rail snapped. Great chunks crushed the deck.

Everyone worked at top speed to get supplies off the doomed ship. In the midst of their work and above the sound of the groaning ship and moving ice, came a strange, terrifying noise. Worsley, on the bridge, turned around quickly and the hair on the back of his neck rose. All hands stopped work. The noise continued; it was like the wailing of ghosts, the cry of mourners at a funeral.

"There!" someone shouted. "Look there!"

On the ice, not a hundred feet from the *Endurance*, stood a number of emperor penguins. They were watching the ship intently and crying out in tones no man had ever heard before. It was as if they sensed the ship was going down, that all was lost.

Frightened by the unearthly sound, the men fell silent. McLeod, a fireman, finally cried out, "Do you hear that? None of us will get back to our homes again."

At that moment it seemed McLeod's words were prophetic.

The cool voice of Frank Wild broke the spell. "You

won't get home if you stand there gaping. Get the dogs off."

One by one the men turned away from the strange sight and went back to work. Dogs were led to the rail but they were so frightened by the strange sounds and motions they refused to leave the ship. Wild quickly rigged a canvas chute. He began throwing the dogs into it. They slid, howling and whimpering, to the ice and scrambled to their feet, shivering.

Water filled all the lower holds and flooded the Ritz. Great needles and pinnacles of ice speared the ship — some passing completely through one side and out the other. A mast toppled with a crash and the ice-covered rigging clattered on the broken deck.

Even the polar veterans, watching the floes grind into the ship, felt hope fading. After 281 days aboard the icebound *Endurance,* after all their work and hope and cheerful spirit, they were done for. They were adrift on the Antarctic ice. The nearest human settlement lay more than a thousand miles away. No one in the outside world knew where they were. There was no hope of rescue.

four
ON THE PACK ICE

THE men stood on the ice, bewildered and numbed by shock. The interminable grinding of floes and the crash of breaking wood in the *Endurance* filled their ears.

The bright sun disappeared behind a scud of dark clouds. The wind returned. It whined through the tangled rigging of the broken ship. A sledge dog howled.

In little groups, the men of the *Endurance* stared at their ship. She had been their safe home, their protection from the freezing temperatures, the darkness and the loneliness of the Antarctic wastes. Now she quivered and shook and fell apart before their eyes.

Worsley loved his small ship with a Skipper's sentiment. Seeing her destroyed moved him more than it did the others. Of all the men Wild appeared least shocked by events. He stood to one side reflectively smoking his pipe, eyes narrowed against the rising wind, waiting for the next move.

Shackleton rounded the ice-covered bow and walked toward the men. They turned instinctively to him. He put his hands on his hips and looked appraisingly at the faces before him.

When he spoke, his words were simple. "We're in a spot," he said. "But we're going to get out of it. Before I tell you what the plan is, I want to thank you for the way you've carried on. No men ever did better." He turned his head to include everybody in his glance. "Now. As soon as we're ready we're going to sledge across this ice to Paulet Island. There's a hut there — and supplies." A faint smile touched his face. "I know they're there. Don't worry about that. I ordered them for Nordenskjöld's 1902 expedition. So that's where we're going. It's about three hundred and fifty miles. Let's make camp and then get ready to travel."

The men looked at one another. The bewilderment gradually left their faces. Shackleton's matter-of-fact tone had calmed and reassured the men — just as he had hoped it would.

The motionless groups of men dissolved. Men

hauled sledges to a large floe near the ship. Wild and the other drivers harnessed the dogs and began to pull the sledges on which the three lifeboats were loaded. The sound of a hammer and cold chisel cutting metal rang out as Charlie Green, the cook, worked to make a stove from an empty oil drum. When the sledges were in place, some of the men stayed to pitch tents; others went to lend a hand to the dog teams as they pulled the boat sledges. Smoke from the stove drifted away on the wind. The sun lowered to the horizon. Finally the panting dogs were unharnessed and staked out in a line across the ice. When they had been fed they curled up in the snow and went to sleep. The Antarctic twilight deepened.

Men still were busy getting their gear into tents when the cry "Hoosh-O" rang out from the "kitchen." Greenhorns like Blackboro stopped work and looked up, puzzled. It didn't take them long to understand what the call meant. Crean and Cheetham grabbed plates and spoons and ran toward the stove. Blackboro followed them.

As they were waiting to be served, Blackboro nudged Cheetham. "Where'd that word come from? Hoosh?"

Cheetham shrugged and a smile creased his weather-beaten face. "Dunno," he said. "Mebbe Nansen. Mebbe Scott. Mebbe the Boss. Could be any of 'em."

"When did you first hear it?" Blackboro asked.

"Oh, back with Scott the first he came down. Then with the Boss in the *Nimrod* and with Scott again five years ago."

"You were with Scott when he died?"

Cheetham shook his head. "I came down on relief." He pointed to Crean, a tall, rawboned, horse-faced man whose ears stuck out from his head. "He found Scott under the snow."

The men jostled in line toward the hoosh pot. Blackboro was silent a moment. "But why do you keep coming back?" he asked. "I'd think once was enough."

Cheetham looked at the youngster in amazement; then his mouth set in a hard line. "I like it," he said, holding his plate out to the cook. When it was filled he grunted and turned away, tramping across the snow to a bit of ice. He sat down, a short, square man, and began to eat with angry motions of his arm. When he'd finished he scrubbed his plate with snow, stuck his spoon in his pocket and lit a cigarette. Then he stood up and looked fondly across the white, God-forsaken wasteland to the still visible horizon.

"Bloody young squirt," he said under his breath. "He don't know what it's like."

When darkness came the men gathered around the lighted stove. Standing apart from the group, Shackleton observed them carefully. Were they in good spirits? Could they endure what lay ahead?

As he stood there Shackleton felt the ice move under his feet. He looked quickly around and saw a crack opening in the ice by the tents. He gave the alarm and everyone ran for dogs, tents, sledges and boats. In a moment camp was struck. The men struggled in the darkness toward a larger floe where once more they put up tents and staked out the dogs.

Wet and weary they crawled into their tents and pushed themselves into their sleeping bags. The dogs curled up in the snow again and went to sleep. Soon the only sounds were an occasional curse from a weary, water-soaked man, the whimper of a dog, the ceaseless growling of the ice.

In the darkness outside his tent, Shackleton paced up and down thinking, planning and watching the condition of the ice. Through an occasional break in the low scudding clouds stars gleamed down on the solitary, moving figure. Midnight came. At the sharp snap of a floe he peered at the surface in the darkness and saw their campground was breaking up once more. He blew his alarm whistle and the men struggled to move camp again.

By the time they had reached safer ice they were too tired to raise the tents, so they crawled under them into their sleeping bags to try to get one more hour's rest before daybreak.

When the eastern sky showed light, the only movement in camp was the hunched figure of Shackleton, still pacing the ice watching over his men.

A movement from beneath a collapsed tent caught Shackleton's eye. He stopped walking to watch the first man struggle out of the debris. There was a muffled curse, a great shaking of equipment and then a head emerged. Frank Wild greeted the new day. His first act was to stick his pipe in his mouth and light it. Only then did he stand up and offer a cheery good morning to the Boss. A few moments later Hurley crawled out and walked over to the two men, his eyes still half-closed.

Shackleton motioned the two men to follow him and they made their way over the ice to the ship. A few moments' search produced an overlooked tin of fuel oil. They carried it back to camp and soon the stove was alight. They melted snow and added dried milk.

When the hot drink was ready Shackleton carried the pan and Wild took a dipper as they went to each huddle of men. Wild woke them with cheerful kicks and calls. He waited as they struggled beneath the canvas and propped the tents up temporarily on the poles. The men inside groaned and cursed their wet, weary state. When they realized a hot drink was waiting for them, eager hands emerged holding cups. The filled cups were instantly withdrawn to the shelter of the tent. No word of thanks came from anyone. When he'd finished serving them all — and had received no appreciation for the gesture — Wild yanked his pipe out of his mouth and yelled, "If any of you gentlemen would like his boots cleaned, just put them outside."

There was a moment of silence. Then, inside one tent, a man snickered; another guffawed. Soon all were up and out, ready for the work ahead. While they produced order from the chaos of their gear, Shackleton scouted around to find a safer floe. When he found one he felt would do, he returned and the camp was moved to the new site. Tents went up.

The cook planted the stove near the center of the floe. Lifeboats on their sledges formed one end of the camp. The men took emergency rations from the sledges, the dogs were harnessed and began a series of trips back to the ship for supplies. Soon piles of boxes littered the camp site. Lumber torn from the ship formed a stack near the boats. As the pile grew, the men christened their temporary home Dump Camp.

Morale was high. The men had a plan for escape from the ice. They had dogs to pull sledges. They had a leader they trusted.

Then Shackleton called the men together. "Get rid of all but two pounds of your personal things," he ordered. "We can't carry everything."

The men looked at each other in silence. Knowing how difficult it was to part with personal treasures and the mementos of home and family, Shackleton pulled several gold sovereigns from one pocket. He reached into another and took out his watch. With one motion he threw them away into the soft snow.

"Two pounds is all," he said. "We're traveling light."

For several hours men could be seen sorting over their belongings. Hurley, who had salvaged all the photographs of the expedition, sat glumly on a hummock looking at his prize pictures, selecting those he wanted most and smashing the plates of the others lest he change his mind. Hussey, the meteorologist, wandered about cradling his banjo in his arms. Sensing his predicament, and knowing music in the days to come would help morale, Shackleton told him to keep the banjo. Wild didn't have so much trouble. He kept his diary, his pipe and as much tobacco as he could find.

Shackleton himself sat a little apart from the men on a bit of ice holding a Bible in his hands. He wanted to keep it but it alone weighed more than two pounds. He finally tore two pages from the Book of Job — one of which contained the verses:

Out of whose womb came the ice?
And the hoary frost of heaven, who hath gendered it?
The waters are hid as with a stone
And the face of the deep is frozen.

Next he tore out the page containing the twenty-third Psalm — his favorite. Lastly he tore out the fly-leaf on which Queen Alexandra had inscribed a parting message:

For the crew of the *Endurance*
from Alexandra
July 31, 1914
May the Lord help you to do your duty and guide
you through all dangers on land and sea.
"May you see the works of the Lord and all His
wonders in the deep."

Shackleton folded the pages and put them in his
pocket. The rest of the heavy Bible he buried in the
ice.

Their decisions made, men fell to work loading
sledges. Dogs were harnessed and lifeboats lashed
to the heaviest sledges. Shackleton and three men
scouted ahead looking for a route across the ice. They
chipped away hummocks to make a path for the following loads. Many times they sank to their knees in
soft snow. The men behind, struggling with the
sledges, sank to their waists in the rotting ice. Time
after time the men had to halt to repair the sledges
which were collapsing under the weight of the boats.
The loads were so great and the snow so soft that it
took all available men and dogs hauling to move one
sledge. After they'd pulled one ahead of the others,
all would return and pick up the lines to another

sledge. That day they moved a scant mile and a half from Dump Camp.

As darkness came on, Shackleton looked from atop an ice hummock for a suitable floe on which to spend the night. From his perch he could see nothing but hummocky ice in most directions. On nearby floes snow — soft and melting — covered the whole surface, making them impossible camping places. Directly ahead was young ice, hard enough and clear of snow, but only two to three feet thick.

He didn't like that ice but he had no choice. So the men, bone-tired, dragged the boats and sledges onto the thin ice and pitched their tents. The cook set up the oil drum stove and soon smoke from the fire drifted out across the darkening sky. The tired men were content to wait for supper but Shackleton, worried about the ice, walked to the nearest lead of open water and tested the edge.

Suddenly a whale rose to the surface blowing, and then sounded. Another and another rose and disappeared. Shackleton stepped back, more concerned than before.

Wild sauntered over and looked at the herd of whales. The men did not speak for several minutes.

The ice quivered beneath their feet as the creatures rubbed against the underside of the floe.

They were killer whales and they were not mis-named. Thirty feet long, weighing several tons and armed with sharp, well-developed teeth, the killer whale is a voracious hunter. Both Wild and Shackleton knew a favorite trick of the killer was to spot a seal or another animal on a thin ice floe, then sound and rush upward, breaking the floe with its back to catch the animal as it floundered in the water. They also knew that if these killers were hungry and saw the nearby camp, they could crack the floe like peanut brittle and then feed leisurely on the dogs and men as they struggled in the water.

"I wish we could move to a thicker floe," Shackleton said. "If there were one where we could camp, I'd do it. No matter how tired the men are."

"Well, there isn't one around here we can use," Wild said. Then he added, "May be an interesting night."

When they got back to the fire, snow had begun to fall — wet and melting in the Antarctic summer night.

The men slept heavily in the darkness, drugged by

exhaustion, but Shackleton only dozed. He could hear the whales still blowing in the nearby open water and from time to time he felt the movement of water and the bump of a whale's back on the ice less than a yard beneath him. The snow slapped his tent as the wind began to rise. In the morning a full-size blizzard whipped across the ice. There was no possibility of resuming their march until the weather cleared.

Wild, Worsley and Shackleton got together in one tent to discuss a course of action. Cradling his pipe in his hand, Wild said, "Figuring the distance we can make relaying in a day, and the food we can carry, we can't get to Paulet. The boats are holding us up."

"But we can't leave them," Worsley protested. "They're our last chance when we get to open water."

Shackleton thought silently a moment, his brow furrowed. Then his face cleared. "We won't sledge it," he said. "The thing to do is camp on the ice and let the drift take us to land or open sea."

Wild nodded but said, "The men. They won't like that."

"They'll take it," Worsley broke in. "I them are optimistic about things."

Shackleton's face hardened. "They've damn well got to be optimistic," he said. "Wild and I will look for a decent floe. When we get back we'll tell them what the new plan is."

The two men walked away into the falling snow to find a safer camp site. After several hours searching they found it — an old floe nearly ten feet thick. From marks on its edges and the condition of the surface, Shackleton knew it had survived two or more years in the pack and probably would last several more before breaking apart.

Men and dogs dragged sledges and boats the few hundred yards to the floe. Ocean Camp was established.

On the soft surface of the ice the men tried to make themselves comfortable. Summer had come and, at first, thoughts of warmer weather cheered the men. But everywhere they turned there seemed to be melting ice or snow. Sleeping bags were soaked. Boots were so wet they squished as the men walked about all day. At night they froze. To thaw the boots every morning, the men held them next to their bare skin until their body warmth turned the icy crust to water again.

Day after day more soft snow fell, melting during the day, freezing into a thin crust at night. On the few days that the sun shone the men hung their clothes, sleeping bags and tents in the steady wind where they could be at least partially dried.

Sledge teams brought more supplies from Dump Camp. When all salvageable material was at Ocean Camp, parties returned to the ship, still visible across the ice. The hull lay low in the ice now; all masts had fallen. She was no longer a ship — only a wreck being devoured slowly by the ice. Water filled all the holds. To get supplies the men had to chop holes in the deck-planking and for hours fish with boat-hooks.

As a snagged box came to the surface the men gathered around to see what surprise package they'd got. A case of tinned Irish stew brought a great cheer from the group. A box of useless soda crystals drew a groan. Loudest cries came when Worsley's full-dress naval uniform popped to the surface — dress coat, trousers, hat and sword belt. Delighted, Worsley took his regalia to camp. That night Shackleton put on the water-soaked uniform, stuck a shovel in the sword belt and strode up and down the line of tents to the cheers of the men.

Camped within sight of the ship, the men felt somehow that all was not lost. Though wrecked, the *Endurance* remained a symbol of safety. It was as though they were camping just outside their home. Yet each man knew the ship could not stay above the ice forever. Early on the morning of November 21st, the floes took a final grip on the shattered hull. Roused by Shackleton's call, the men came from their tents and stood in small groups, watching the ship in its final struggle. Slowly, the stern rose in the air, and black water closed over the ship. She was gone below the ice, to the dark sea floor forever.

No one spoke. There was little to say. Finally Shackleton said sadly, "She's gone, boys," and turned away.

Dejection settled over the men. They had lived over nine months in the icebound ship. They had escaped from her when she was crushed. They had started to sledge out but that plan of escape had to be abandoned. Now they were alone in the icy desert on rotting ice — as lost as men ever have been. Each move they made seemed to take them nearer death.

Worsley, Wild and Shackleton walked away from the men. Shackleton looked back at them and said, "I'm going to hoist the King's flag tomorrow. It'll cheer them up. Especially as the King presented it to us."

"I don't suppose the King would recognize you now," Worsley said, laughing. "You must have looked different when you had that audience at Buckingham Palace."

Shackleton grinned and the lines of worry and strain disappeared from his face. "You mean the King wouldn't want to know me now?" Then he laughed. "I don't suppose he thought when we were talking that I'd ever find myself in this pickle."

That night, in a more reflective mood, Shackleton talked with Worsley about the war. "I wonder, Skipper," he said, "whether you fellows wouldn't have been safer in a man-of-war after all?"

Watching Shackleton's anxious face, Worsley sensed the guilt the Boss felt at bringing his men into such danger.

"Don't worry," he said lightly. "We'll probably get back in time to see a spot of war anyhow. Things look pretty bad at the moment, but we'll come through.

Anyway," he added, smiling, "if we don't get home, the experience alone will have been worth while."

Shackleton laughed. He clapped Worsley on the back and looked at Wild who sat cross-legged on the water-soaked tent floor mending a sock with a rusty needle and a bit of thread.

They had lost everything — the ship, the chance for success of the expedition — and they were in danger of losing their lives.

In the morning Shackleton had a long pole rigged on the wooden lookout station near the tents and as the men stood ankle-deep in the slush of the Antarctic snow, he hoisted the Union Jack. It unfurled in the wind and snapped back and forth.

It was a solemn moment, a break in the routine, one that called for some celebration, so Shackleton issued one can of the salvaged stew to each man and they all poured their ration into the cooking pot. The cook fired up the rickety oil drum stove and as the smoke stung their eyes the men stood as close as they could to get at least one side of their bodies warm and partially dry. Soon the first bubble rose to the surface, then another and another. The men's mouths began to water. They sniffed the savory dish and stood closer, each gripping his spoon and cup, waiting eagerly for his portion. Finally the cook stepped forward and, like a bandleader, flourished his dipper once above his head and reached for the first helping. As his dipper sank beneath the appetizing surface of the stew, the bottom fell out of the stove.

A moment of stunned silence was broken by a loud groan from the men — so loud the dogs in the snow stood up, their hackles bristling in excitement. The men dived to retrieve whatever they could. Lucky ones got bits of meat and potatoes. The less fortunate came up with pieces of blubber fuel and charcoal.

Each clear day Worsley climbed the lookout station and took a sun sight while the men, in a circle below, waited for him to announce how far they'd drifted north. The ice drift was erratic. Some days they moved north toward open water, on others wind drove the floe south again. Not all days were stormy. Occasionally the sun rose in a clear sky and then the grandeur of the Antarctic was evident. Great tabular icebergs sparkled in the sun. Sounds on the cold, windless air carried so well that men talking a mile and a half away could be heard in camp. Despite being continually water-soaked, no man was sick in the germ-free atmosphere. In the rays of a setting sun the distant ice appeared pink and mauve, the shadows blue and violet.

Much as they welcomed clear days for drying clothes, the men welcomed a blizzard from the south since it increased their northward drift. The floe was now in a position where they had alternative goals. Paulet Island remained a possibility. But there was also Snow Hill Island and Wilhelmina Bay where whalers sometimes came in the summer. If they could reach that bay they might be rescued.

To prepare for the coming boat journey, Shackleton had the carpenter raise the gunwales of the boats for added protection in the open sea. The men rigged sails with any material at hand. The activity and prospect of leaving the ice so excited Shackleton that with Worsley and Wild he talked for hours at night planning an expedition to Alaska. To him there was nothing incongruous about sitting on a rotting ice floe in the Antarctic, lost and in danger, planning another adventure, dreaming another dream.

Of all the men, Shackleton suffered most from inactivity. Impatient, impulsive, longing for progress, he paced endlessly up and down on the floe. Only those who knew him well realized how much it cost him to conceal his frustration. Wild knew — and Worsley. While talking one evening, Wild glimpsed on an open page of Shackleton's journal the words "Waiting! Waiting! Waiting!" Above that: "I pray God I can manage to get the whole party to civilization."

As the ice began to break, Shackleton warned the men not to stray from the large floe on which they'd camped. He forbade hunting seals and penguins unless they appeared close to camp. But boredom and monotony gripped the men. When the Boss's back was turned they skied off behind hummocks playing hooky on the broken ice. They used small floes as ferries and their ski poles as paddles to get across leads. Even dog teams and sledges made forbidden trips from camp. Drivers would get up all possible speed on a big floe, hit the brash ice and hope to get to the next floe before losing momentum and sinking into the water. Sometimes they didn't make it. Then dogs, men and sledge would have to be hauled from the freezing water.

A few days before Christmas, Shackleton decided to start sledging again across the ice. He felt that any progress toward their goal, however small, was better than more inactivity. The men loaded sledges and secured the boats. The promise of action put everyone in high spirits. Before leaving Ocean Camp they celebrated an early Christmas Day. On December 22nd the men sat down to a feast of stores they could not carry with them. They gorged on ham, sausages, tinned milk, jam, biscuits, coffee, cocoa, pickles, tinned rabbit, peaches, parsnips and baked beans.

Early on the 23rd, after two months of idleness, the journey began again. Shackleton and Wild led the way, chopping lanes through pressure ridges for the passage of the boat sledges. The cook and his helper followed with the stove and fuel aboard a small sledge. Behind came the heavy boats pulled by the men, and the lighter dog-drawn sledges.

Far to the northwest lay land — uninhabited and barren — but safer than the rotting ice across which they were to travel. The waiting was over — or so the men thought.

five
PATIENCE

DURING summer near the Antarctic Circle, the sun does not set for ten weeks. It swings low toward the horizon during the usual hours of darkness and its rays, slanting across the snow and ice, are cooler than at midday. The surface slush freezes and forms a thin crust that makes sledging easier.

To take advantage of this, Shackleton scheduled marching for the "night" hours. Even then the sledges broke the crust. Men fell into holes waist-deep and had to be hauled up by their comrades.

During the day the exhausted men slept in pools and rivulets of water. But soaked, dirty and weary as they were, they remained cheerful as they struggled toward their goal. The soot-blackened cook and his helper, sledging ahead over the spotless snow with the stove, were nicknamed Potash and Perlmutter and it was always a welcome sight to see the two black figures stop, the canvas walls go up and a cloud of blubber smoke come out of the stove — the signal for a brief pause, a hot drink and a small ration of biscuit.

The going was slow. Eighteen men, under Worsley, hauled a boat sledge sixty yards across the ice, then all returned to pick up the lines of the remaining boat sledge. This relaying cut progress to a snail's pace. When they hit hummocks and uphill pulling was necessary, their advance was measured in yards. Five hours of backbreaking work netted two hundred yards toward land.

When they rested, the men's torn and greasy clothes gave little protection against the cold and wet. When they were sweating at the sledge lines, the same clothes seemed unbearably heavy and thick. Under the ever-present sun the men's lips burned and cracked. Their hands chafed and would not heal.

The dogs pulled well. Under skillful drivers, they moved equipment sledges ahead of the boats and waited, panting in the snow, for the boats to catch up. Then one of Wild's best dogs, Blackie, fell lame and had to be shot. He was the first to go.

On the fourth day of travel Shackleton climbed a

small, tilted berg and looked over the "countryside" ahead. To the north and west he saw wide, open leads crisscrossing the floes. He climbed down and motioned Wild to come with him to prospect a safe route. The two men walked ahead without speaking. The only sound was the gurgle and swish of their finnesko boots in the ankle-deep slush, the occasional crack of a floe. When they reached a lead they stopped and squinted across the dark water and ice beyond. As far as they could see the condition persisted. Silently Shackleton pointed to the least hazardous route — a steppingstone course from floe to floe. It would make progress even slower but it was the only way.

They went back and picked up the traces of the lead sledge. The men fell into place and the long, slow march resumed. There was little joking now. Short rations had weakened them. More and more men had to harness up to the sledge traces to move the precious boats.

On the seventh day Worsley scrambled up an ice hummock and took a sun shot with his sextant. Below him, sitting or lying on the ice, the men waited and watched the Skipper wondering what progress they had made. They had struggled over the worst ice in the world under the worst conditions. They knew they were closer to their goal than they'd been at Ocean Camp. The question was: how much closer?

Worsley finished taking his reading and climbed down, his face expressionless. He talked with Shackleton in a low voice and then turned to give the men the news. In seven days of marching they had moved a scant ten miles.

The men received the news silently. Some bowed their heads in weariness and momentary despair. At that rate it would take nearly three hundred days to reach the nearest land. South Georgia still was a thousand miles to the north. With only forty days' emergency rations on their sledges Paulet Island or any other land was out of reach. Grimly Shackleton ordered the march abandoned. The men moved the sledges back to a large floe, losing a hard-won half mile. They staked out the dogs and fed them. The stove was lighted and a mug of thin cocoa given each man. As the sun lowered in the sky its rays struck the threadbare walls of the small huddle of tents. Patience Camp was established.

The name was not a joke. They all needed patience now. The only course left to Shackleton — the one he had to take — was to wait and hope the ice would drift to the open sea or land. They could do nothing but conserve their food and strength — and wait some more.

Hope of survival was small — even the hope of making slight progress toward a goal. All the resources of their spirits had to be called on. Day followed day in the white wasteland with nothing happening to renew the hope of survival. They knew that friends at home considered them dead. The struggle over the ice, the semi-starvation rations had weakened them. Nerves became frayed. Tempers flared. Some men refused to leave their tents.

Shackleton billeted his men in the tents according to their temperaments — which he had studied closely. From time to time he shifted them around to prevent cliques from forming. He knew they had to remain one in spirit and action or all was lost.

As for himself, Shackleton went among his men with every show of confidence. He joked whenever he could discover anything to joke about. The wisdom of letting Hussey keep his banjo now became apparent. It provided music and the men sang. They sang of home, of firesides, of warmth and cheer and somehow, in that death-dealing wilderness, a part of each song's warmth reached them.

As the will to live in some of his men dwindled, Shackleton deliberately started arguments to rouse them. The subject didn't matter. He grabbed any chance to get a spark of response from them. The differences between the Greek Orthodox Church and the Roman Catholic Church brought on strong words one day — blood pressures went up, the men bristled — Shackleton walked away, smiling to himself. Behind him they still argued, but now they stood up like men, determined to win a point. Another time the argument was over currency. To settle it the men consulted one of the torn volumes of the *Encyclopedia Britannica* they'd salvaged. That book proved both sides wrong. Angrily, the men united and condemned the accuracy of the sacred reference.

Worsley produced three decks of cards salvaged from the lost ship. One deck belonged to Shackleton. When Worsley presented it, Shackleton riffled the cards with his cracked, dirty fingers and began to play bridge with all comers. In addition to his bridge tournaments, he played several hands of poker each afternoon with Hurley. That became a ritual, an island of habit and order in the middle of chaos. Each day he seated himself on the ice and dealt the cards on a scrap of canvas. Hurley would pick up his cards, sneak a look at them and begin to bet. Stakes ran high and the game was a masterly display of card-playing technique. Day after day the contest continued. Hurley's winnings piled up. It was a fearsome struggle. At the end of ten weeks the game still was going strong.

To his delight Hurley had won a shaving glass, several top hats, enough walking sticks to equip a regiment, assorted sets of cuff links plus an entire library of books. In addition, he had dined, at Shackleton's expense, at Claridge's in London and had a good night at the opera in a box seat.

Shackleton had his winnings, too. He'd been Hurley's guest at the Savoy, visited most of the London theaters, won a lifetime store of linen handkerchiefs, silk umbrellas, a mirror and a rare, collector's copy of *Paradise Regained* — a book he'd always wanted.

The one activity everyone enjoyed was hunting seals and penguins. These two animals are the only worthwhile game in the Antarctic. One seal will yield 800 to 1000 pounds of meat and blubber. Unafraid of man, they do not flee when approached. The difficulty lay in getting the killed animal back to camp. Leads opened and closed around every floe;

the surface was soft and pools were filled with broken, brashy ice. All these things hindered a sledge's progress. Fearful of his men's lives, Shackleton warned them not to hunt too far from camp and never alone. Ice conditions could never be counted on and should a lone hunter get into trouble by himself he'd have no hope of rescue.

All the men didn't share his concern, however, and on many occasions his rules were broken. Orde-Lees, the motor expert of the now motorless expedition, skied one day across several ice-filled pools scouting for seal. He didn't take a gun. Three floes from camp he saw a dark motionless shape on the ice ahead. As he watched, the animal stirred, raised its head and stared at him. Lees had never seen a seal like it before. There was something different about its coat which was brown with a pattern of spots of darker color. Its muzzle was thin. The head had a predatory shape. Lees stopped fifty yards from the seal and they eyed each other. Suddenly the animal moved — not away from Lees but toward him. Its thin lips curled back and showed a strange set of fangs — long and cruel.

Lees turned and skied for his life. He knew he had stumbled across a sea leopard, not a placid

Weddell or crabeater seal. He'd heard stories of carniverous sea leopards and as he hurried away he realized his danger. The animal attacks anything that moves on the ice. It has no natural enemy and hence no fear. It will eat fish, seals, penguins — or men.

Lees's skis sank into the surface ice and seemed to stick there. His legs moved but with the clogged, taffy motions of a nightmare escape. He dared not look to see if the sea leopard were gaining. But it was. The animal moved gracefully and rapidly over the soft ice, slithering up and down hummocks, his eyes fixed on his prey. At the edge of a floe the sea leopard dived into the water and swam ahead beneath the ice to cut off Lees's escape. Lees frantically hurried on. He stopped as the sea leopard's head appeared in front of him, dripping wet at the ice edge, waiting. Lees saw the unblinking, intelligent eyes of the creature staring at him. He turned at right angles to his course and skied across the floe away from the animal. It dived again to cut off Lees's escape.

Frank Wild, watching from camp, saw Lees's predicament. Without wasting a motion, the normally quiet, taciturn Wild uncoiled. He picked up a rifle and ran toward the two figures, shouting, swearing at all greenhorns in general and Lees in particular.

At Wild's approach the sea leopard turned, attracted by the noise, and looked at him. With no hesitation the animal abandoned its chase of Lees and charged Wild.

Wild stopped and raised his rifle. He waited until the onrushing beast was within a few yards of him. He fired once. The bullet hit the sea leopard between the eyes. Its undulating movements stopped as it rolled dead at Wild's feet.

Shaken, Lees helped Wild drag the sea leopard into camp. When they cut it open they found in its stomach fur from the bodies of several seals. The sea leopard was skinned and its body cut up and frozen for future rations.

Moments of excitement came infrequently, however, and the men had to fight the deadliest of all circumstances: monotony.

The one unspoken preoccupation of everyone was the rate of drift toward the north and west — toward land. On each clear day Worsley climbed the lookout tower to get a sun sight. He took binoculars with his sextant and under the pretext of looking for seal on the ice he stared to the west, trying to spot land amid the large bergs above the mirage-struck horizon. February passed into March and March brought blizzards and storms. Winter was coming. The men sat huddled in their tents — now worn and dotted with holes which let in the wind — keeping their hands against their bodies for warmth. They talked of many things but principally of food, mountains of their favorite dishes: puddings, roasts, bread and butter, gallons of hot drinks, ale, champagne, dumplings, stews, pies and cakes.

As their rations were cut further the men lived on what seal and penguin meat they could get. One by one the dogs were shot, skinned and stewed. Blubber from seals, which turned the men's stomachs before, was now eaten greedily. Seal oil — as thick and black as train oil — was a delicacy. They drank it as though it were nectar. The supply of blubber for fuel was diminishing. They used up the last of the cocoa. Dried milk mixed with water from melted ice was their only hot drink; their only food became one biscuit or small pancake per day. For drinking water, ice chips were put in cups and these were held against the men's bare skin until their body warmth turned the ice to water.

Thin and weak, they slept in puddles of melted surface ice, never dry, never comfortable. When southern winds howled across the ice, the temperature dropped swiftly and everything froze solid. Blankets became as stiff as sheets of iron.

Through all this time Shackleton sat either in his tent or outside on the ice, externally calm, playing bridge with the men, playing poker with Hurley —waiting.

In warm weather the snow became so soft the men could not walk standing up. When they emerged from their tents they had to crawl on hands and knees to the kitchen for their small daily ration and return the same way to their tents. The last of the dogs was shot and eaten.

In early April, seals and penguins became more scarce as they migrated farther north. To replenish supplies, the men had to hunt farther and farther from camp. Shackleton would not let the less adept greenhorns go out at all. Oftentimes he himself went accompanied by Cheetham and Worsley. One day, on such a hunt, Worsley spotted several penguins on a distant floe. The three men began dragging the sledge across open, narrow leads and pools filled with small floe bits to get within range. Four penguins were shot and loaded on the sledge but during the return trip, as they were ferrying the sledge across a pool on a small floe, a killer whale blew in a nearby pool. Its ugly snout rose high above the water. Silently the three men paddled faster across the pool. All knew what could happen if the killer saw them. The whale surfaced again, closer this time. The small floe they were on came to a stop against brash ice nine feet from the edge of a thick, safe floe. Cheetham and Worsley scrambled across and began to haul the sledge. Shackleton stayed to guide the sledge and hold the ferry floe steady by paddling with a ski pole. They could hear the killer now as it rose and blew again, nearer than before. The sledge was pulled to safe ice but, as Shackleton prepared to make a running jump, wind took the small floe back out into the pool. He paddled desperately with the ski pole while Worsley and Cheetham stood watching, holding their breaths, not daring to speak.

Moments seemed hours as Shackleton struggled to bring the floe back into position. The edge ground against the brash ice. Shackleton threw the pole across and, running hard, scrambled the last few feet to safety.

Both Cheetham and Worsley knew how narrow the escape had been — not just for Shackleton, but for all of them. With Shackleton lost, their chances of survival would have dropped nearly to zero.

None among them had his experience in dealing with the Antarctic. None had the quickness to handle emergencies instantly and with assurance. To many men it seemed that "Canny Jack" Shackleton rode strictly on luck. To those who knew him well it was plain he had thought out, long years before, each possibility, each conceivable disaster with a corresponding plan of action to meet it. He was at his best, intelligent and strong, fighting his most cherished adversary: the Antarctic. He lived for little else.

While others slept, Shackleton thought and planned. He lay awake or, more characteristically, paced restlessly outside his tent. Through his mind went hundreds of possible accidents and he mentally solved them all. So intense was his concentration that even while he slept the contest went on. Often at night he would wake from a nightmare — one involving danger to his men. He would cry out and sit up, roused by the dream of losing a man. When he realized it was a nightmare, he would remain awake, while he searched his mind for a way to solve the imaginary crisis. Only when he was satisfied with a solution would he lie back and close his eyes once more.

All the time Shackleton schemed to conquer the Antarctic, he remained cheerful, determined and optimistic. Never for an instant would he publicly admit the possibility of defeat. His buoyancy and determination infected his men — even the most dispirited of them. It carried them all. He cajoled, joked, argued, prodded, pushed and led them all the time. He shared their rations, their hardships, their games and songs. He was one of them, yet always ahead of them, leading them on.

Neither Worsley nor Cheetham spoke of the narrow escape as the three men dragged the sledge back to camp. Words were useless.

The nights became longer and darker. Storm winds from the south drove the floe northward. Throughout the storms the men stayed in their tents, emerging only for food. The temperature dropped and tent mates huddled together for warmth. Wind whistled through the worn canvas walls. Snow drifted over everything. During one such storm the floe traveled eighty-four miles northward and crossed the Antarctic Circle at last. Weak but cheerful, the men stood outside their tents when the wind died and looked around. The camp floe was smaller. It had been chipped and worn by the action of the sea and surrounding ice. In the distance great flat-topped bergs shone in the sun. They were typical icebergs of the Antarctic, split off in sharp, rectangular shapes from the ice shelf far to the south. Some were huge ice islands, several miles long and wide. They rose sixty or seventy feet above the water and extended far below the surface. To whalemen headed south these bergs are outposts of the Antarctic. To the starved men of the expedition who viewed them now they were heralds of the open sea to the north.

Shackleton stood with his men admiring the great bergs. But where they saw only the shimmering white mass, he saw danger. As the sun sank toward the horizon and the brief day ended, he ordered each man to stow rations in his pockets. He set watches that night. During the darkness a wind sprang up — a north wind. The giant bergs, two of them close to Patience Camp, began to move in response to the unseasonal wind. As dawn broke they were much closer, their sheer white sides towering over the pack. The wind increased. Suddenly the men too became aware of the danger. The bergs, weighing over a million tons apiece, began to bear down on the hapless group. Patience Camp lay directly in their path. No human force could divert them. Quietly, Shackleton moved among the men telling them to abandon the sledges with their final rations, abandon everything except the clothes they wore and the food in their pockets.

The wind increased. The bergs picked up speed, plowing through the pack, tearing ice apart as though it were tissue paper. Hummocks were tossed on the approaching faces of the ice cliffs like sticks, crowding higher and higher until they fell with a splintering crash into the sea. Behind the bergs lay miles of broken, tossing brash ice, little bits on which no group of men could live. The roar was thunderous as the bergs moved in a straight line toward the men. The group stood silently, watching the mist of white powered snow and ice form a halo over the gigantic ice mountains.

Never had they seen the irresistible force of Nature in so concentrated a form. Few, if any of them, could survive the impact. Somehow they felt cheated. They had struggled to survive so long. But mingled with the sense of loss there was a sense of awe. If they had to die, they were aware that it would be no mean death at the hands of such an adversary.

Worsley moved to Shackleton's side. Shackleton shouted something. Worsley bent closer to catch the Boss's final words through the roar of splitting ice.

"Have you got a light?" Shackleton yelled.

Worsley handed him a match and watched as he struck it with his thumbnail. Shackleton nodded his thanks and then watched the oncoming icebergs while he smoked his cigarette.

six
ESCAPE

SNOW driven from the icebergs now formed a white shroud that wrapped the men. The noise was so great no one could make himself heard — if he had wanted to speak. Beneath their feet the floe trembled. The men's faces were white; they stood paralyzed as they saw death approaching.

A scant few yards away, the bergs veered suddenly and passed by, leaving in their wake roiled water and churned bits of broken ice. The camp floe rose and fell on great swells, and the rotten ice on its edges broke off in a number of places. But Patience Camp was left intact.

Silently Shackleton turned away from the sight, finished his cigarette and walked toward the deserted kitchen. The men returned to their chores — the endless sewing up of tattered clothes, the lighting of the cookstove fire, the melting of a bit of ice for a few drops of water. Darkness fell. Hussey's banjo came out and its plunk, plunk, plunk drifted out across the ice. When the meager ration that was their supper had been eaten, they went gratefully into the tents, pushed themselves into their wet sleeping bags and fell asleep. Death had never been closer.

The next morning Worsley climbed the lookout platform and took a sight. Clouds were blowing up from the south. Another blizzard was on its way. Wind whistled through the platform supports and whipped the worn flag back and forth. Worsley braced himself and took his reading. When he came down and finished his calculations, he announced they were as far north as Paulet Island but sixty miles east of it. Shackleton shook his head gloomily. It might as well be six hundred miles for the good it did them. The ice between the men and land was broken and loose. No boats could survive in the leads or small pools which opened and closed at the caprice of the current. No sledges could cross from floe to floe.

Snow fell so thickly the camp could not be seen from thirty yards away. The men chopped bits of ice for drinking water from the ice surface, put them in tin cups, grabbed a few biscuits and crawled into the tents. The blizzard howled down on them.

For six days it snowed and the wind blew with hurricane force. As they lay waiting and talking in the tents, the men were thankful for only one thing — the hurricane was driving them north. When at last the wind died, the men crawled out and began shoveling four feet of snow from around the stove, the supplies and sledges. It was the morning of March 23rd. Worsley climbed stiffly to the lookout tower again and scanned the northwest horizon through his binoculars. He stared for a long time, took the binoculars from his eyes and stared without their help. He called to Shackleton who climbed up and looked too. Then Wild and Hussey went up. The remaining men gathered anxiously at the foot of the platform. The men on the tower talked in low tones; then Shackleton climbed down. "We're in sight of land," he said. "Have a look."

Stunned, almost unbelieving, the men climbed hummocks and crowded up the ladder to the tower one after another to see. On the horizon they saw a towering mass. At first many thought it was simply another berg, but the mass had black streaks down its sides. It was somewhat conically shaped — unlike the usual flat-topped bergs of the Antarctic.

"It's Mount Percy," Worsley called out, "on Joinville Island."

Pandemonium broke. They were sure now. The confirmation of sighted land was enough. They milled about on the small floe shaking one another by the hand. They had not set foot on land for over fifteen months. Now it lay within sight. Smiles lighted the bearded, blackened faces. Questions flew thick and fast. How far away was it? How long would it take to get there? When would they start?

They no longer doubted they would survive. Whatever its condition, it was land and they would soon have solid earth under foot once again. In their minds it seemed but a step from that barren shore back to the broad green fields of England — and home.

Even Wild and Worsley grinned with relief and expectation. Once more Shackleton and Worsley climbed the tower and looked at the northernmost tip of the Antarctic continent.

"Will you try for it tomorrow?" Worsley asked.

Shackleton gazed silently north for a long time.

Worsley became uneasy. He moved restlessly back and forth on the windswept platform.

"No," Shackleton said at last.

Even Worsley's broad shoulders drooped when he heard the answer. Like the men, he'd been so overjoyed by the sight of land he hadn't stopped to analyze their position.

Shackleton turned to him. "I can't risk crossing this ice," he said. "It'll be opening and closing all the time. The boats might get crushed. We might be separated. A lot could happen."

"You're right," Worsley agreed gloomily. "It would be terrible if anything happened now, after two thousand miles on the ice."

Shackleton's face brightened. "If we keep on as we are for another hundred miles or so we're bound to drift into open water. Then we'll make for the nearest whaling station."

Worsley simply nodded, to hide his disappointment.

Shackleton climbed down to the men waiting below. Their faces were turned toward him; they were almost leaning forward in their anxiety to be up and away across the ice to land.

"We can't go now," Shackleton said quietly. "We must drift farther north, to open water."

For a moment the men couldn't comprehend his words. When they did, their faces showed first disbelief, then anger — then despair. Some of them wandered dazed across the ice. Others stood silently, gripping their hands, unable or unwilling to speak.

To many it seemed Shackleton was condemning them to wander in the desolation of the ice pack until their food was gone and death mercifully put an end to their struggle. Yet even now, none questioned him; none wavered.

By the end of March, Joinville Island was out of sight to the south of Patience Camp and Mount Haddington, on James Ross Island with its snow-covered slopes which had offered hope of a landing, was only a memory. Conferring with Wild and Worsley, Shackleton spread out the worn and greasy chart on the tent floor.

"The best thing to do," he said, "is to head for Clarence or Elephant Island. They're a hundred miles due north now. We're moving steadily toward them. If we miss them . . ." He shrugged. "Well, then we'll have to try to make South Georgia."

His finger moved slowly north and east across the chart, away from the land which lay to the west — so near and yet so far against the current — out across the South Atlantic Ocean to the small dot that was South Georgia. It lay eight hundred miles out to sea — a freezing, stormy sea of forty-foot waves and heaving pieces of ice.

Shackleton's pointing finger stopped at South Georgia but his glance moved on to the nearly three thousand miles of uninterrupted ocean beyond.

"If we miss South Georgia," he said, "if the wind and currents take us beyond it, we can't turn back."

After a glance at his two lieutenants' faces, Shackleton went on, more cheerfully. He pointed to land lying west of Clarence and Elephant Islands. "That's Deception Island," he said. "We could make it there from our first landfall. In good weather we could go from island to island across the top of Graham Land and come out all right."

"Why Deception?" Wild asked, squinting at the chart.

"According to Admiralty Sailing Directions there are emergency stores there," Shackleton said. "And whalers call in November. All we'd have to do is wait."

Wind from the south blew steadily all the while now. The floe was moving toward open sea as Shackleton had predicted. There were signs of progress all around. The ice was looser. Their floe was whittled away by contact with neighboring floes and by the action of water on its rotting sides.

Early in April, Shackleton stood near the edge of the floe looking north in the dim twilight. He seemed to be waiting for something, some signal. Each evening he went there and stood a few moments and then returned. This day, as he stood spraddle-legged on the floe, he smiled. He felt the floe rise slightly and fall away, rise again and drop. It was what he'd been waiting for: the long, rhythmic swell that came from the open ocean beyond the horizon. The time to leave the ice was near. He returned to camp and ordered the boats prepared.

To the men the boats represented their one remaining chance for survival. They had dragged them slowly and painfully from the *Endurance*, then to Ocean Camp and on to Patience Camp. When they'd been straining at the traces the boats seemed mountainous objects, incapable of being moved without the most exhausting effort, as solid and heavy as bergs. But as the time for launching approached, the men eyed the thin wooden hulls with different feeling. Against the backdrop of crashing, heaving ice, their boats appeared as fragile as glass, as light and frail as toys.

The longest, the *James Caird*, measured just over twenty-two feet. The *Dudley Docker* and *Stancomb-Wills* were heavier but not so long. Shackleton was to command the *James Caird*. In it were Wild and eleven others, plus the greater part of the stores. Worsley was to skipper the *Dudley Docker* with nine men aboard. Hudson and Crean were senior men on the *Stancomb-Wills*.

The men stood watches around the clock as the threat of the ice breaking increased. It rose and fell heavily in response to the ocean swell running beneath it. The camp floe was a long narrow one, as solid as any in the pack. But it shifted and presented its shorter dimension to the oncoming seas. It began to pitch like a ship. When the swell was directly beneath the middle, both ends rose unsupported from the water.

On April 8th the floe cracked straight across beneath the *James Caird*. The alarm whistle brought everyone from his tent to move boats and supplies to the larger piece of the floe during the moments when the two pieces crashed together. Finally men and equipment were safely aboard the larger piece of floe. Standing near the edge, Shackleton saw the split had passed directly beneath his tent site. The hollow which his body had pressed in the ice over the months was cut in half. The place where his head and shoulders had rested was on one piece of ice; the indentation made by his legs and feet was on the other.

That night the men feasted on seal meat and all other food they couldn't take in the boats. Watching them, Shackleton knew they'd have need of all the energy they could get for the sea journey ahead. Inactivity and short rations had sapped their strength. He wanted them at least to start with full bellies.

The next day everyone stood waiting quietly by the boats watching the leads open and close around them. Ocean swell ground ice edges together and each man, watching the action, knew perfectly well what would happen if a boat were caught even for an instant between two walls of closing ice.

Shackleton studied the pack ahead, measuring the chances. At one in the afternoon the leads became wider and stayed open. A few miles away was a large open pool nearly three miles in diameter. Shackleton turned to the waiting men and gave the signal. The *Dudley Docker* and *Stancomb-Wills* slid off the edge of the floe six feet down into the water with a great splash. Some of the men jumped aboard immediately. Others handed supplies from the ice to the waiting hands in the boats. In a few moments the crews were all aboard and Shackleton ordered the two boats away. The men rowed toward the large open pool.

The *James Caird*, the last boat, had to be launched loaded. It went over the ice edge, splashed into the water, rocked crazily back and forth and then righted itself. Shackleton and the men scrambled down. Oars went out and the men began to pull away down a navigable lead. From his boat Worsley looked back for one last glance at their "home" of so many months. It lay a mile astern but he still could see the abandoned equipment and stores, black dots on the unfriendly ice.

Shackleton, in the *James Caird*, took the lead; the other boats followed in train as the expedition worked its way between the chunks of moving ice toward the distant pool. Sails were useless since the masts didn't rise above the ice surface so the men were forced to row. Oars dipped in and out of the ocean. As wet blades rose in the cold air the water on them froze instantly. Each dip brought more water, more ice. The spray splashing on the gunwales froze and the boats sank deeper in the water. From time to time the men had to ship oars and hack off the ice with spoons and pocketknives. Progress was slow.

Shackleton's boat rounded a floe and the large pool opened before it. The men bent their backs pulling against the swell to reach the comparative safety of ice-free water. Standing in the stern, Shackleton looked ahead. From one side of the pool he saw rushing toward them a tide rip carrying great pieces of ice. His oarsmen also saw the danger and by hard rowing pulled the *James Caird* clear. But the men in the following boats were unaware of the danger. The wave could swamp the boats; the ice could crush them.

Shackleton pointed to the wave. "Pull!" he shouted. "Pull hard!" Then he could do nothing but watch as the other boats struggled to escape the wave.

seven
THE FREEZING SEA

WORSLEY and Crean, at the tillers of the trailing boats, looked in the direction Shackleton was pointing. Instantly they understood the danger. Their shouts roused the oarsmen who pulled with all the strength in their weakened bodies. Slowly the boats responded and moved forward trying to outrace the approaching wave. Then the swell bore them upward to the crest. Further efforts of the men seemed useless as they all felt the great force of the moving water beneath them. When it passed, the men rested on their oars, exhausted. But the boats were intact.

When Shackleton saw everyone was safe he turned his anxious gaze north, across the open pool, to find a route through the loose pack ice. In the pool's center floated a large tabular berg. Rowing to windward of it the men gazed in awe as swells broke against the lofty, blue-white tower of ice sending spray sixty feet into the air where it caught the sun's rays and fell back, a shower of rainbow-colored drops.

At the other side of the pool Shackleton saw a wide break between two floes. He set a course to northwest. He planned to clear the northern edge of the pack and head west for Deception Island. A fair easterly wind helped them on. When darkness came Shackleton picked out a large floe for the night camp. The boats were hauled up on the ice, tents erected and the stove lighted. Soon the smell of cooking rose in the air. The men sang and joked in their tents while Shackleton wrote up his log. A sense of accomplishment pervaded the camp that night. Whatever lay ahead they were on the move, doing more than simply waiting for the drifting ice to decide their fates.

The date was April 9, 1916. Nearly a year and a half had passed since they had sailed from South Georgia in the *Endurance*.

After a meal and a smoke, the men turned in. Within minutes they were sound asleep. The floe heaved and tossed beneath them. The watchman strained his eyes in the darkness to see what lay around the floe. From time to time he kicked at the rotting ice and walked back and forth to look for cracks. He found nothing to cause alarm. The grinding of the floes, the whistle of the wind and the splash of waves breaking against the ice were the only sounds that kept him company in the night.

At eleven something wakened Shackleton. He didn't know what it was but it had signaled danger to him even in his sleep. Wide awake, he listened intently to every sound — the wind, the flapping tent sides, the creak of the ice. He crawled out of the tent and started to walk toward the watchman at the far end of the floe.

Without warning the floe broke beneath one of the tents. The canvas sides stretched as the ice separated beneath the sleeping men, then they ripped apart. Shackleton shouted and dragged the sleeping men from the edge of the ice.

"Man in the water!" someone shouted.

Before anyone else could move Shackleton dropped to his knees on the edge of the floe and reached down into the sea. He felt the bulky shape of a sleeping bag in which someone, still half asleep, was trapped. He grabbed the bag with the one hand and pulled upward, putting all the strength of his body into the motion. The bag came up with the man in it. Shackleton rolled the rescued seaman onto the ice as the edges of the broken floe slammed together closing the crack momentarily.

The rescued man was Holness, a fireman. He sat on the ice, safe but soaked. His principal complaint was that his precious tobacco was wet.

While Holness shivered and grumbled, the others transferred all supplies to the larger piece of the floe. When the last tent and boat had been safely passed over, Shackleton found himself alone on the small bit of floe in the darkness. Before he could leap across, the current shifted and began to carry the floe away from the men. He lost sight of the others in the darkness and shouted to Wild to launch a boat. But Wild has seen his predicament and already was pushing the boat into the water to rescue the Boss. In a few minutes Wild and Shackleton were back, and the boat was secured again.

Even though everyone was safe temporarily, their position was critical. At any time the small camp floe might be crushed by larger floes or tossed in the path of unseen moving bergs. They could not risk falling asleep again that night.

Shackleton ordered milk heated and served to all hands. The men gathered about the lighted stove. Their bearded, greasy faces gleamed in the light. Hands scarred by frostbite clutched the rusted tin cups. But one man could not join the half-warmed group. Holness had no dry clothes to wear after his dunking. To keep from freezing, he ran back and forth across the little floe, his jacket and trousers cracking as the ice formed and broke off. Teeth chattering and bones aching, he had to keep moving throughout the rest of the night.

Daylight came slowly on the morning of April 10th. Hot hoosh was served. Then the men waited impatiently for the signal to launch boats. At eight the order came. The boats splashed into the icy water. Once more the little fleet sailed north, struggling to break out of the ice into the open sea.

The wind still blew from the east. If it held until they reached open water, they could run before it toward Deception Island. Luckily, leads to the north stayed open and by noon the boats were clear of the pack. But as they moved out into the winter seas, waves began to pour over the gunwales. Crests thirty and forty feet high tossed the boats about as though they were chips of wood. The wind freshened. Icy spray stung the men's faces. After months on the flat, stable ice the violent, irregular lurching of the boat made some of the men seasick. They lay groaning, soaked with water in the bottom of the boats while the others bailed desperately.

Shackleton saw it was hopeless to travel with such a high sea running. He turned the boats back and they ran for the shelter of the hated ice. It had the effect of a reef, moderating the seas, and once within the pack the men managed to bail the boats dry.

Shackleton knew the men were nearing exhaustion. So at three-thirty in the afternoon he ordered boats hauled up on a floe. Hot milk, hoosh and sleep were needed. For the next twelve hours all talk of sailing stopped.

As dawn came on April 11th, Shackleton looked hopefully to the north. During the night the pack had closed around their floe, pinning them once again in the ice. Every few minutes Worsley, Wild, or Shackleton trudged to the highest point — a fifteen-foot ice ridge — and searched for an approaching lead or pool. After anxious hours Shackleton saw a dark spot of open water. Driven by loose ice, the camp floe drew nearer the pool. Shackleton saw a wide navigable lead stretching away from one side of it to the southwest. It was not the direction they wanted to go; but they had no choice. They could only go where the navigable leads pointed. The three fragile craft slid down the steep side of the floe; supplies were dropped into them. The men scrambled off the ice edge into the boats again. Oars beat out a steady rhythm. Once more the soaked and weary expedition was on its way.

When the boats reached the wide lead, sail was raised and they moved rapidly over the open water. Killer whales surfaced beside the boats. Overhead flew screaming petrels, Cape pigeons and skua gulls. The expedition was near open ocean once again.

But dusk came before the ice was left behind. The boats were tied to the only large floe in sight. Its sides were too high to permit hauling the boats up. While the boat commanders stayed aboard fending the ice away from the gunwales, the men climbed up on the floe and got hot food from the stove that had been set up. Before they clambered again into the boats Shackleton ordered a further reduction in gear and supplies. In the heavy sea outside the pack ice, a deep-riding boat could founder in a minute.

Since leaving the *Endurance,* so many months ago, the men had abandoned surplus gear several times. They stripped now to the absolute minimum for survival. From now on the loss of anything could jeopardize their lives. When they had finished they got back in the boats and the long night vigil began. Floes and smaller bits of ice loomed in the night, swept along by wind and current. The men fended the ice away as best they could and waited for daylight. Amid the jostling, breaking ice they could hear the explosive hiss of killer whales, blowing all night long. Ghostly forms of birds flashed by, their white bodies appearing then disappearing quickly in the darkness.

The morning of April 12th came clear and bright. The wind dropped. As the daylight made things visible, Shackleton looked around at his men, gauging the additional stress they could stand, watching for signs of collapse. Their faces were thin and gray, fatigue drew heavy lines in the cheeks of even the youngest members of the crew. But when Shackleton's glance traveled back to Wild, he almost smiled. His second-in-command sat, as he had all night, holding the tiller firmly, pipe gripped in his teeth, his blue eyes looking forward eagerly to the new day. Of all the expedition members, he alone showed no sign of strain.

Beyond the ice pack the men saw the blue of the open ocean. White crests of waves glittered in the morning sun. With hopes high, the men raised sail and the boats moved to the west. Since April 9th they had had a good easterly wind and should have made good progress. At noon Worsley scrambled forward in his boat to take a sight. He stood on the gunwale, wrapped one arm around the mast and took his reading skillfully while the boat rose and fell on the water. Then he worked his way aft and began to calculate the position. Shackleton drew his boat alongside Worsley's and jumped aboard.

"How are we doing, Skipper?" Shackleton asked as he looked over his navigator's shoulder.

Worsley finished his calculations and handed the position, written on a scrap of paper, to the Boss. Shackleton looked at it and frowned in disbelief. Then his face brightened and he motioned for his boat to come alongside. When he was aboard the *James Caird* again, one of the men shouted, "Are we making it, Boss?"

Shackleton smiled. "Not as much westing as I'd hoped," he called.

He had to say something. But how could he tell the men, wet and weary as they were, that a current from the west had overcome the fair winds and driven them thirty miles to the east of their original position? They actually had lost distance since they'd first launched boats. Deception Island was farther away than ever.

It seemed to Shackleton now that Deception Island as a landfall was out of the question. Without hesitation he changed course to the southwest, making for Hope Bay on the mainland of the long arm of the Antarctic continent now eighty miles away. With sail set they moved forward until darkness again overtook them. At dusk Shackleton headed again for the shelter of the pack but the running sea had set the fringes of the great belt of ice into violent motion. No boat, small or large, could enter it. He sent Worsley ahead in the *Dudley Docker* to scout a large berg and see if the boats could find shelter to leeward of the ice mountain for the night. On returning, Worsley reported that swells were hurling brash ice against the side of the berg. No safety could be found there. Desperately the men pulled their boats toward a large free piece of ice two miles away and made fast to its side. But the running sea gave them no rest. The waves were so violent that the cookstove couldn't be hauled to the ice to heat food. Small Primus stoves were lighted in the boats and a little milk warmed for the men. Darkness fell. More and more ice began to crunch against the thin sides of the boats. The boats themselves banged into each other in the heavy seas. Finally Shackleton ordered the boats slacked off in the darkness and they drifted away from the ice, tied together by lines. Lookouts were set to warn of approaching ice. The men strained their eyes in the darkness to spot the glimmer that would be the first sign of floes or bergs bearing down on them. The temperature dropped to an estimated four degrees below zero. Spray, splashing on the boats, froze. The men's beards turned white with frost. All night long they huddled together for warmth, not daring to move, whispering each to each his thoughts and fears. Spray froze on their jackets, encasing them in ice. Later, the moon broke through the scudding winter clouds and snow showers fell from the clearing skies. The boats bobbed slowly up and down on the freezing seas, three small, white objects lost on the face of the subantarctic sea carrying twenty-eight freezing, starving men.

When daylight finally came on April 13th, Shackleton anxiously scanned the faces of his crew. Where they had shown fatigue before, they now seemed worn to the point of collapse. He knew they had to make landfall soon or the weaker ones would die in the boats.

During the night their path toward Hope Bay had been blocked by ice, cutting them off from that landfall. In addition, the wind had shifted. It now blew fair for Elephant or Clarence Island to the north.

Shackleton ordered cold rations passed to the men for breakfast. Then he got Worsley aboard his boat. He told Wild and the Skipper of his new plan; make straight for Elephant Island — one hundred miles across the wave-tossed sea. The men who could work distributed stores equally among the boats. Then they raised all possible sail and the three boats ran free through the loose pack ice. Each boat had a man at the bow with an oar to clear ice from the boat's path. Desperate now, Shackleton let the boats go as fast as the wind could carry them. Ice bumped and scraped against the hulls. A piece of floe pierced the thin side of the *James Caird*. Fortunately, the hole was above the water line.

The wind rose to hurricane force blowing the boats faster and faster toward open water. About noon they reached the edge of the pack once more and plunged boldly into the wild sea. Like impudent cockleshells, the three small craft rose on each mammoth wave, lurched on the crest, and swooped to the trough on the other side. Despite high wind the sun shone on the scarred, bearded faces of the men. Blue water roiled around them as they held a straight course for safety.

At dusk Worsley ran his boat alongside Shackleton's and, shouting, asked if they could sail on through the night. But already the other boat, the *Stancomb-Wills,* was scarcely visible among the waves in the gathering darkness. Shackleton vetoed Worsley's scheme. The one thing he feared most was their separation. So, despite the agony and weakness of the men, he ordered sails furled.

A sea anchor was fashioned from oars and the boats tied together behind it, bow to stern. Darkness fell. More cold rations were passed from hand to hand. The men tried to eat them but salt spray had worked into their cracked and chafed lips. Their mouths were swollen so that they couldn't eat, despite their hunger. Seasickness kept some from even trying. The temperature dropped far below freezing. The boats sank lower in the water from the added weight of ice forming on the gunwales, masts and thwarts. Wearily, the men chipped at it, tossing chunks over the side only to see more form as they worked.

Thirst began to plague the men. The boats had left the ice pack in such a rush that no one had paused to haul aboard fresh ice. The last piece, a puny ten-pound chunk, was broken up and passed among the twenty-eight men. Relief that came from sucking the ice was offset by increased soreness of their lips and the unavoidable reduction of body heat.

All that night Shackleton sat at the tiller, one hand holding the painter attaching the *James Caird* to the trailing boat. As the line dipped in and out of the sea it grew heavy with ice. He expected it to part at any minute, but it held.

The men huddled together again for warmth. From time to time they looked longingly toward their sleeping bags which were stowed in the bow beneath an unbreakable sheath of ice. The seasick men lay as though dead in the bottom of the boat. Diarrhea and dysentery made their condition and the state of the boat unbelievably foul. Able men sat on the thwarts shifting from side to side to trim the boat as great waves rolled out of the blackness on one side, struck them and disappeared, leaving behind a wake of froth and roiled water. Others bailed all night long to keep the boat from foundering.

As the night hours passed, Shackleton hailed the other boats to learn the condition of the men. It was much the same as in the *James Caird*. Once he called in the darkness and from the *Stancomb-Wills* came the answer: "We're doing all right." Then, plaintively, "But I would like some dry mitts."

Dawn of April 14th came clear. The morning sunlight turned the sky pink, and far to the north the rocky peaks of Elephant Island rose above the horizon. The wind dropped to a moderate southwest breeze. All hands worked quickly to clear ice from the boats. The sea anchor was hauled in but could not be brought aboard. Ice had sheathed the oars so thickly they were now the size of telegraph poles. Leaning over the gunwales, the men hacked the ice away and at last drew the precious oars into the boat.

Before setting sail Shackleton passed out frozen sealmeat for breakfast. But it was not food the men needed now. The curse of shipwrecked sailors was close on them: thirst. From their bits of sealmeat the men sucked out blood greedily — cracked lips or no. But in a short while the saltiness of the blood brought their thirst back with redoubled fury. Shackleton gave orders to the other boat commanders that sealmeat was to be passed out only at stated intervals.

The little fleet set out once more. In everyone's heart was the hope that this day would be their last on the ocean, that by nightfall they would have land once more beneath their feet.

Seasickness, dysentery, diarrhea, thirst, hunger and frostbite rode that day with the expedition.

Late in the afternoon the wind shifted. It blew against the ocean current, setting up a severe choppy wave pattern. The boats sailed as close to the wind as possible but their progress was slow. Oars were run out and the weakened men pulled as best they could toward the land that now seemed so close. But darkness came again before they reached it. Some of the men sat staring at the cliffs and glaciers with tears in their eyes. Others showed no emotion at all; some cursed silently and hopelessly as another terrible night overtook them. Shackleton brought the *James Caird* alongside the *Dudley Docker* and the *Stancomb-Wills,* tending the men, trying to cheer them. He couldn't expect them all to live.

As darkness came, the *Stancomb-Wills* was taken

in tow by the *James Caird*. The smaller boat couldn't carry as much sail as Shackleton's and it tended to lag behind the others. Sailing as close together as possible, the three boats worked toward land in the darkness. The wind rose to storm force again. The able men began to bail faster as water poured in. Later, Worsley's boat came alongside the *James Caird* again. Worsley asked if he could go ahead to scout a landing place.

"All right!" Shackleton shouted, "but don't get out of touch."

Worsley waved and nodded. The *Dudley Docker* fell away. A snow squall blinded Shackleton for a few minutes. When the squall ended, the *Dudley Docker* was no longer in sight.

All night long Shackleton flashed a lamp on the sail of the *James Caird* and peered into the blackness for an answering gleam that would tell him of the safety of the other boat. He saw nothing. The wind howled its dirgelike tone as it swept the crests from the waves and sent blinding spume flying through the air.

What Shackleton feared most — the separation of the boats — had happened.

When the *Dudley Docker* fell away from Shackleton's boat, Worsley was not particularly concerned. The snow squall obliterated the other boats but he kept his course. After the squall passed he saw the flare of the lamp on the sail of the *James Caird* and, lighting a candle to shine through the tent rigged over the bow, he answered. But he had no way of knowing Shackleton could not see it.

Worsley's boat compass had been smashed and the only means of navigating was by his small pocket compass. He got the direction of the wind — west shifting to southwest — and the direction of their landfall — northwest. With the compass held in one hand, he settled down at the tiller for another night on the hurricane-swept ocean. To get his men's minds off their thirst, he passed the candle lamp among them so they could light their pipes.

Midnight passed. The *Dudley Docker* entered a tide rip running off the southeast corner of the island. This, plus the counterrunning seas, made the boat ship more water over bow, stern and beam. Orde-Lees began bailing steadily. The cold, though not so intense as before, was still twenty degrees below freezing. Although all sail was up, oars went out to steady the boat and correct the course throughout the night. McLeod and Cheetham manned the oars, spelled occasionally by Greenstreet.

As Worsley handled the tiller, straining to see the onrushing waves, Cheetham, pipe in his mouth, rowed. When his pipe went out he'd call to Worsley for a match.

"Haven't got many dry ones," Worsley shouted above the wind.

Cheetham pulled a moment in grumpy silence. "Pay you a bottle of champagne for a match. Come by when I get my pub started. I'll make it good."

Swearing, Worsley handed over a match.

Later there was need for yet another match. Another bottle of champagne was credited to Worsley's account. So the two men passed the night at the height of a storm on the winter ocean.

After midnight Greenstreet's foot suddenly became numb with frostbite and he had to stop rowing. Lees took the frostbitten foot and warmed it the only way he could: by raising his sweater and holding the frozen foot against the skin of his stomach.

At 3 A.M., his foot partially unfrozen, Greenstreet went aft to relieve Worsley at the tiller. During the nightmare of the past days the men had got what rest they could by dozing on the bottom of the pitching, tossing, befouled boat. But Shackleton, Wild, Worsley, Crean and Hudson, commanders and seconds of the boats, had not slept for a hundred and eight hours. When Greenstreet pulled Worsley away from the tiller, the Skipper couldn't straighten up. He was so cramped from the cold and wet that he was bent double. The men pulled him forward and began rubbing his stomach, thighs and groin to restore circulation. When he could move under his own power, Worsley stumbled forward to the unaccustomed luxury of an hour's nap before returning to the tiller.

When daylight came, Worsley saw his boat was close to the cliffs of Elephant Island. The light increased and the men scanned the ocean for sight of another boat. But mist and sea fog shrouded everything beyond a few hundred yards. They saw nothing but rolling waves, cliffs and swooping gulls.

Elephant Island lies north of the topmost land of the Antarctic continent, $61°05'S$, $55°10'W$. To occasional whalers who pass by, it presents a hostile appearance. In places along its coast, cliffs rise directly from the sea's edge, vertical and unscalable, to form snow-covered mountain peaks. Ice sheets curl down over the black rocks. In breaks between them glaciers push down to the sea's edge. The ocean is never quiet. Surf crashes on the vertical shore or spews upward as swells surge over uncharted reefs. No ship attempts to land; no man had ever set foot on Elephant Island.

Worsley sailed by the alien cliffs, close to the great white glaciers. He wanted a place to land — but first he wanted water. Some of his men were going mad. Ignoring the danger of ice falling from the glacier face, he sailed boldly toward the only source of fresh water. The men leaned from the boat and hauled in precious chunks of glacier ice. Ignoring the coating of salt, they broke them apart and sucked the ice greedily. The boat lay to for an hour while the wonderful melting ice flowed down parched throats. The salt burned their sore lips, the ice itself made their mouths and throats ache more. They didn't care.

When the worst pangs had been eased, Worsley steered on around the island in search of a beach. The mist thinned and the fog blew out to sea. Scanning the coast ahead, Worsley saw what appeared to be a narrow channel through a reef that lay close inshore. Waves boomed across the dangerous spine of rock, sending showers of spray high into the air. Beyond, he saw, or thought he saw, a narrow, rocky beach lying beneath the jutting cliffs and an overhanging glacier. In a lifetime spent at sea he had looked on more favorable beaches but none had looked so good as this one did now. He steered the boat for the channel.

To his amazement and delight he saw the other two boats trying to get through the same channel ahead of him. So great was their relief that everyone in Worsley's boat stood up, waving and cheering.

None of the men in the boats ahead could hear their calls. The sound of water crashing over the rocks drowned all other sounds, and their own predicament took all their attention. Standing in the *James Caird*, Shackleton watched the water boiling through the gap in the rocks. He knew he could lose boats right here on the verge of safety — and men would die.

Transferring himself to the *Stancomb-Wills* — the more lightly laden boat — he ordered it through the channel while the *James Caird* stood offshore. A great wave took the small boat and hurled it through the channel, barely missing the rocks. Riding the wave crest, the *Stancomb-Wills* raced forward past the reef and ground to a stop as the wave crashed on the beach. The next wave moved it farther toward safety.

Elated, Shackleton turned and grinned at his men. His glance happened to fall on Blackboro whose feet were so frostbitten he could not stand. Determined to give the young man the honor of being the first human being to touch the island, but, forgetting in his exuberance all about the steward's frostbitten feet, Shackleton knocked Blackboro overboard. Before Blackboro could protest, he sank, spluttering and helpless, into the icy surf. Frantically, Shackleton and others leaped out and pulled him clear of the waves.

The men quickly unloaded the *Stancomb-Wills* and shoved off to get some of the *James Caird*'s cargo. Then both boats came to land. Finally Worsley's boat shot through the channel and at last all were ashore.

The men walked or crawled about the beach. Some were dazed beyond speech; some looked at that bleak spot with tears of thankfulness in their eyes. Others reached down and picked up rocks, gripping them hard in disbelief. After 496 days of living on ship, ice and raging ocean, they had solid ground underfoot at last.

Shackleton himself was almost carried away by elation. At that moment he didn't notice the state of the beach, nor did he pause to appraise their situation. His eyes were on his men. "Thank God," he said fervently, "I haven't lost any of them yet."

Frank Wild brought him back to earth. That small man stepped out of his boat, walked gingerly across the rocks glancing nonchalantly at the cliffs, the glacier behind them and the frothing sea almost at their feet. Despite his rags and tatters, his beard and grime, he somehow managed to give the impression of an Englishmen out for a stroll in a London park. He stopped a few feet from Shackleton and lit his pipe. Then he stepped over beside the Boss and, leaning forward, spoke above the roar of the surf. "I think we'll find the weather here simply appalling," he announced companionably, with a slight nod of his head.

eight
THE INHOSPITABLE ISLAND

WORSLEY began immediately to inspect the beach. He walked to the cliff a short way from the water and examined the rocks carefully. There was no break in them that would permit the men to go inland to a safer camp site. Worse, his experienced eye saw tide marks and evidence of erosion caused by sea ice on the cliff high above his head.

He turned and looked at the sea. Heavy surf broke on the rocky beach. Water spouted over the reef offshore. Beyond that lay floating bergs, floes and, in the distance, the ice pack.

The beach was no haven. At any moment a sudden storm could sweep boats, men and stores to oblivion. They were no safer here than in the open boats — in many ways not as safe.

Worsley went to tell Shackleton what he had discovered. In the fading light Shackleton's appearance startled him. He seemed to have aged many years during the days at sea. His shoulders sagged. He seemed ready to drop from fatigue. Deep lines had appeared in the corners of his mouth, and his hair and beard were white with sea spray. Worsley remembered all the times during past months when everyone had slept while Shackleton paced the ice, watchful and awake. He remembered the constant alertness, the effort to ease everyone's burden — and Shackleton's words: "If I lose any of them I'll feel like a murderer."

Now, seeing the effects of the responsibility of such leadership, deeply felt and impossible to share, Worsley marveled again at Shackleton's strength.

"What do you think, Skipper?" Shackleton asked, nodding toward the cliff.

Worsley shrugged. This certainly was no time for a pessimistic answer. He spoke in a casual tone but chose his words carefully. "It isn't the Riviera," he said. Then he pointed to two seals lying on distant rocks. "Plenty of grub though," he added.

For the first time in many days Shackleton laughed. It seemed to relieve his strain and weariness a little.

At that moment the cry "Lunch-O" rang from the cookstove. Shackleton clapped both Wild and Worsley on the back and moved toward the food with some of his old quickness.

A seal had been shot, skinned and cut up. As fast as the cook could turn them out, steaks went hot and smoking to the men's mouths. They alternated the lean meat with strips of blubber. Melted glacier ice provided a limitless supply of fresh water. It was a banquet.

When the men had eaten all they could hold, they fell to work putting up the ragged tents, drawing the boats beyond the reach of the surf and stacking supplies at the foot of the cliffs. When they'd finished they went back to the stove and began eating again.

Darkness came before the last man had eaten his fill. Weary beyond belief, the men struggled into the tents and pushed themselves into their sleeping bags. Rocks pressed into their backs and legs and arms. There were no complaints. Each jab and push of a stone was a reminder that they had reached land safely at last.

Shackleton got into his sleeping bag and, for the first time since launching boats from Patience Camp six days before, closed his eyes for a night's sleep. He didn't stir for twelve hours.

In the morning he woke before the others and began to explore the beach himself. He scrambled over rocks to the cliff base, walked along the impenetrable wall to the glacier hoping to find access to the interior. When he returned he was frowning.

He called Wild and Worsley aside for consultation. Like Worsley he was aware of the danger. He'd seen the tide and ice marks on the cliff. He also reported finding large jagged pieces of rock near the cliff — giant stone chips that had fallen from the cliff face recently. The dilemma was plain. If they moved camp as far from the water as possible they'd be in danger of falling rocks. Yet even if they took that chance they weren't safe from storm waves or spring tides.

There was one thing to do: find another beach. After breakfast, Wild, with Marston, Crean, Vincent and McCarthy, set sail in one of the boats to explore farther along the coast to the northeast side of the island.

Shackleton and Hurley tramped for miles along the beach over rocks and ice to search for a pathway inland. But they failed.

While the search went on that day the other men rested. They produced salt-crusted, rusty needles and rubbed them on rocks until they were bright once more. Then, with bits of thread, they relaxed mending the remnants of their gear — and eating. There seemed no end to their appetites. At the stove, Green served meals all day long. Though he was exhausted he remained cheerful, working all day.

Evening came. Wild's boat had not returned. Anxiously, Shackleton paced the shore. He ordered a flare lit and placed on a rock.

Though they were on land, Shackleton began to doubt that they'd made any real progress toward safety. At sea the men had nearly died from thirst; the boats had escaped foundering by a narrow margin. It was true they had water here and solid earth under their feet. But where, exactly, were they? On a rim of nameless beach so situated that it could be swept by waves which could finish them all in an instant. As he paced the shore Shackleton began once more to analyze their whole effort to survive in the light of these new circumstances. Winter was on its way; seals and penguins — their only source of fresh food — soon would become scarce as the animals migrated north. The ice pack would come then, crashing, crowding on the narrow shore.

While walking and mentally calculating what to do, Shackleton kept his eyes on the darkening sea. Twilight had given way to complete darkness and he found himself peering into the night, squinting to catch a glimpse of Wild's boat.

At eight o'clock a pale, ghostly shape loomed on the waves outside the reef. Shackleton stopped pacing and shouted. In a moment the boat, with Wild and the others safe aboard, shot through the channel on a wave. Eager hands pulled it out of reach of the surf.

Cheerful as ever, Wild stepped out. There was a beach, he reported, farther along the coast — a 200-yard strip of rock and sand that ended in a rocky point well out from the cliffs. Best of all, some of the rocky ledges definitely lay above the highest tides or storm waves. He was sure of that, for the high rocks held a penguin rookery. Beyond that beach, though, interminable cliffs rose straight up from the sea for a thousand feet.

The news cheered everyone although it was too late to make the move that night. When they'd eaten again they turned in gratefully — chancing another night on the dangerous beach.

Privately Shackleton worried. The weather had been relatively calm during the last thirty-six hours. Of one thing he was certain: it wouldn't stay calm long at that latitude during that time of year.

By morning a strong current was sweeping ice floes and bergs rapidly along the coast just offshore. Beyond the relatively narrow stretch of open water and moving ice was the pack itself, nearing the island. If it reached shore before the men could launch boats, they would be held prisoners for days or even weeks.

The men needed no urging. Hastily they ate breakfast and then began loading stores and gear. Still weak, they took longer than they ordinarily would and the task of moving the boats across the rocks to the water seemed gigantic. They had to use oars as rollers, placing them under the keel of one boat at a time. Three oars broke and had to be discarded.

Finally the loaded boats were afloat. The men waded out and climbed in. Pulling hard they rowed through the channel and out beyond the protective reef.

A gust of wind swept down from the cliffs. One instant the air was calm; the next the storm Shackleton had worried about was on them. Within moments a high and dangerous sea was running. The small sails of the boats snapped tight. Wind thrummed through the rigging. Low clouds scudded by overhead.

Under oars and sail, the boats moved slowly against the current, westing around the island. To avoid the driving ice and the full strength of the storm, they stayed as close inshore as possible, dodging reefs, rowing out when the force of wind and waves threatened to dash them on the cliffs.

At one point, under the partial protection of a jutting rock islet, they paused to eat. The men handed cold rations along to their companions. Each move had to be made carefully lest the waves pitch someone overboard. The boats rose and fell on swells that rolled beneath them to thunder and break on the cliff. They were so close inshore that some had to pole the boats off the rocks, using the oars, while others ate as quickly as possible.

The storm had not slackened when they came opposite the beach Wild had discovered. The sea was beaten to a froth; nothing but white water lay between boats and land. But the bows turned shoreward and the men struggled at the oars the last few feet through the surf.

As soon as the bow of each boat touched the shore, men leaped out. Slipping and falling on the rocks, they tugged the heavily laden craft farther up out of the boiling surf. While some held the boats as far up on the beach as possible, others unloaded. As fast as their weakened condition permitted, the men staggered above the reach of the waves, dumped boxes and went back for more.

Rickinson, an engineer, stood panting beside the gunwale of his boat after one trip up the beach when suddenly his face turned white and he collapsed in the water. The men pulled his unconscious body from the surf and carried him to safety. Hastily the two doctors, Macklin and McIlroy, pitched a tent and put the sick man in his sleeping bag. Though conscious by then, Rickinson couldn't move. The months of idleness on the ice, the malnutrition and the sudden heavy work had taken their toll in the form of a heart attack. He lay immobilized while the others went on with the work.

In landing supplies, two of four bags of spare clothing fell into the surf and were lost. Since the men's gear was down to a minimum already, the loss was serious. It certainly would affect their comfort. It could become critical in their survival.

Darkness had fallen by the time all supplies and boats were safely up the beach — and the storm still raged. In a freezing wind of hurricane force the men struggled to pitch tents. They had to remove mittens to fasten lines, and frostbite promptly numbed their fingers. When they'd finished, they ate a brief hot meal, standing in the partial shelter of a few rocks. Snow began to sting their faces as they headed for the shelter of their tents.

At midnight a wave washed into Shackleton's tent. He went outside and saw that the high tide, driven higher by the waves, threatened them again. He blew the alarm whistle and the men came out, half asleep, into the wind and darkness to shift camp. The snow still swirled around them, carried in all directions by the wind eddying about the cliff. The only place above high water was the ledge where the penguins had nested. They had no choice but to camp there.

Though safe, the new location had one terrible drawback. It smelled unbelievably foul from layer on layer of droppings from the birds. By the time the men were in their tents trying to get a few hours sleep, everyone lay in a thick, yellowish mud.

Outside the wind continued to blow. Snow piled thicker and thicker on the windward side of Shackleton's tent. At three in the morning it collapsed and the men with Shackleton lay clutching the lines and tent pole, to keep it from being flung out to sea. Worsley's tent split in two. Grabbing the halves, he and his men overturned one of the boats and crouched, shivering and numb, through the rest of the night. As an added precaution they tied the boat itself down with heavy lines rigged over the upturned keel.

Daylight came slowly. Clouds and the lateness of the season made even midmorning a dim, gray twilight. Snow lashed at everything and the men stayed in their shelters, emerging only for food.

Green, working hard all through that day, finally staggered away from his stove and collapsed on the beach. Half dragging, half lifting him, Shackleton got the cook into a tent. Now two men had suffered heart strain and perhaps were permanent invalids.

The months of exposure and low rations on the pack ice of the Weddell Sea had been lived through — but they began to exact their price. As the men weakened, their desire to live began to fade. One announced he wanted to do nothing but stay in his sleeping bag until death mercifully took him. When the cook collapsed, Shackleton went to that man's tent, yanked him out and informed him he'd just been made cook of the expedition. Drastic as the medicine was, it appeared to work. Within hours after he'd expressed a desire to die, the man was sweating over the stove, worrying intensely about the possibility of a pair of drying socks falling into the hoosh pot.

The Antarctic winter moved closer. The few penguins that remained on the island headed north. Seals became scarce as they too joined the migration to open water. Ice crowded the bleak shore of the island.

Shackleton sent men farther and farther from camp in the eternal search for fresh meat. Often they returned empty-handed. The condition of the men worsened. Apathy and despair settled over the group. The sick did not improve. Blackboro's frostbitten feet got worse and the doctors discussed the amputation of his toes. There was no anesthetic.

Except by extreme rationing, there was not enough food to last through another winter. Their island lay far off the course of any whaler or commercial vessel. No one would think of searching for them on Elephant Island even if it were possible to get through the oncoming ice.

The men had never known such isolation. Into their speech and gestures crept the conviction that they would all die on the inhospitable island.

One cloudy morning Shackleton and Worsley walked to the end of the rocky promontory now named Cape Wild in honor of its discoverer. The walk had become a daily habit. It gave Shackleton a chance to inspect the ice surrounding the island, to look at the weather, scan the shore for seals — and plan the next move.

When the two men were alone, Shackleton said. "Skipper, we'll have to risk the boat journey. I'm not going to let the men starve."

Worsley was silent a moment, squinting into the distance. "Would you let me take the boat?" he asked finally.

"No, that's my job," Shackleton said rather sharply.

But Worsley was stubborn. "I know boats. In fact I've had more small-boat experience than you."

Shackleton shook his head again. But this time he grinned. "Don't worry," he said. "You'll be with me, anyway."

When they walked back to camp, Shackleton called all the able men around him. He spoke briefly, telling them in outline what the situation was as he saw it, and what had to be done in order for them to survive. As he finished speaking he said, "It's a small hope. I don't expect anyone to come who hasn't weighed the chances thoroughly." Then he asked for volunteers.

Without speaking, all the men stepped forward or raised their arms to signify they would take the chance. So Shackleton had his choice of those best fitted by experience and condition to make the attempt with him.

Some of course, had to remain to care for the sick; others, though eager to chance the trip, did not have the training such a voyage required. Shackleton chose his crew carefully.

Worsley was to go as navigator and second-in-command. McNeish, the carpenter, was chosen to apply his skills in keeping the boat afloat. Crean, the indefatigable veteran, joined the group. Lastly,

Shackleton picked Vincent and McCarthy, both strong seamen with experience on North Sea fishing trawlers.

With Shackleton that made six men. Their goal was South Georgia Island, more than eight hundred miles away, across the most stormy seas in the world. Wind and current, sweeping eastward from Cape Horn during the winter, turned the ocean into a vast welter of roiled water. Forty-foot waves rolled across the wastes of the freezing sea. One mistake in navigation would send the boat past the island into the broad reaches of the South Atlantic. If that happened, the boat could not beat back against the strong current and winds. It would be lost. A mistake in handling the boat would be as fatal. The light boat would buckle, capsize or fill with water so cold no man could survive more than a few moments.

But there was no choice. The impossible journey was the only alternative to starvation.

In the dim light of morning, on the wind-swept beach, the men fell to work to prepare the boat for launching. The longest boat, the *James Caird*, was chosen. It was twenty-two and a half feet long. Built according to Worsley's specifications, it was lighter and more buoyant than the ordinary lifeboat. To strengthen it against the pounding of the seas, McNeish took the mast of the *Stancomb-Wills* and secured it inside the *Caird* along the keel. Next, with wood salvaged from the other boats and from supply boxes, he built a deck frame over the gunwales. The only nails came from the supply boxes — and these were so short they scarcely held. While McNeish hammered and sawed, Greenstreet sewed canvas bits together to provide deck covering. A mizzenmast sprouted near the *Caird's* stern. Sails from the other boats were recut and rigged.

Lying on the beach in the driving wind of the past few days hadn't helped the *Caird's* seaworthiness. Daylight showed through opened seams. Patiently McNeish calked the seams with bits of cloth. There was no compound to lay over the calking so, in desperation, he squeezed oil paints from the artist's kit into the cracks. To finish the job in the best possible style, he smeared seal blood over the paint.

While McNeish and some helpers worked on the boat, the others gathered supplies and equipment. Thirty days' food was stacked just out of reach of the tide. A ton of rock ballast was sewn into the few precious spare blankets. Glacier ice, melted down, filled two wooden water casks. To supplement that supply, a 200-pound chunk of ice from the glacier lay beside the stores, ready to go aboard.

All who were able worked. But the tasks of preparation were not uninterrupted. Storms and driving snow often drove the men to the shelter of their tents. When the blizzards ended, they came out, shoveled away snow and fell to work again.

The six men going were outfitted as completely as the remaining store of clothing permitted. Their oilskins and waterproof seaboots had been abandoned long before. But each man wore heavy underwear, trousers and a thick sweater. Each had two pairs of woolen socks covered by reindeer boots that came to the knees. On their hands were a pair of woolen mittens and, on top of those, dogskin mitts. A heavy woolen helmet completed their gear. It was hardly seaman's dress, and certainly it was not waterproof. But it was the best that could be provided.

Navigating instruments, a rifle, sleeping bags, stove and fuel went into the boat. As preparations neared completion, Shackleton drew Frank Wild away from the others to talk over plans for the men remaining behind. Wild was to be in command. Shackleton's instructions were few, for he trusted Wild's judgment and knew that, whatever the circumstances, Wild would do the right thing. In essence, Shackleton told him to reduce rations to get through the winter. If help did not arrive by spring he was to launch the two remaining boats and make for Deception Island.

Both men knew the chance of survival through the approaching winter was small — there simply was not food enough, although the final emergency boat-stores remained intact.

As daylight waned on April 23rd, Shackleton walked to the tip of Cape Wild and estimated the chances of good weather and open water in the morning. The sky was overcast but wind was moderate. Ice was the greatest problem. Heavy floes moved along the shore. Any sudden wind could drive the pack tight against the rocks and cut off escape. Already it was dangerously near.

Returning to camp, Shackleton announced departure time as early on the twenty-fourth as possible. Everything had been done. Delay could be fatal.

That night, under upturned boats, the men smoked and talked after a meager supper. They seemed reluctant to part company and go to their tents and sleeping bags. An air of forced jollity hung in the clouds of tobacco smoke. Doc Macklin swore with gruff affection at everyone. Someone called out in the semidarkness, "If the Skipper's aboard, they won't sink. He wasn't born to be drowned." Wild and Greenstreet periodically reminded Worsley to bring back all the beer he could. But all the jokes and back-clapping could not hide the fact that the hour for the desperate voyage was close and unavoidable.

The morning of the twenty-fourth of April came gray and windy. The men fell to work silently. No smiles or laughter relieved the strain. They launched the *James Caird* empty and began ferrying out supplies in the *Stancomb-Wills*. Stone ballast, food, sleeping bags and ice went on board. The two wooden water casks floated out tied to the stern of the *Stancomb-Wills*. Unnoticed by anyone, a cask struck a submerged rock, cracking the wood and letting in sea water.

The ferrying trips continued. The wind rose and soon a gale was blowing. The swells increased. One caught the *James Caird* and turned it, spilling McNeish and Vincent into the icy water. They struggled ashore and exchanged their soaked clothes for the dry ones of two men in the shore party. There were no spare clothes left. The spill seemed to be a bad omen and the men gloomily completed the task of loading the boat.

On shore for the last time, Shackleton conferred with Wild, talking in low tones. Then he shook hands with each man, not forgetting the sick men in their tents. Blackboro smiled at him and wished him luck. His festering feet lay, useless lumps, beneath the swath of blankets.

Seated in the boat, Worsley somehow didn't want to look back at the men left behind. The pain of leaving friends, perhaps forever, was great.

Men in the *Stancomb-Wills* rowed Shackleton out to the heavily laden *Caird*. He climbed aboard and slowly the little boat worked through the reef channel. The *Stancomb-Wills* followed a short distance, then fell away and returned to the beach. Worsley looked back once over his shoulder at the small figures dwarfed by the towering backdrop of cliffs. He saw their arms wave in a final salute, heard their cheers faintly carried on the wind. Then he heard nothing but the roar of moving ice floes ahead.

nine
THE ONE CHANCE TAKEN

TWO problems faced the men in the *Caird* when they left Elephant Island. The first was to keep the boat afloat; the second was to survive while doing it.

Originally, the *James Caird* had been well built. But dragging it across pack ice and beaching it on the rocks had weakened the fragile hull. Bumping into loose bits of ice produced leaks immediately. The ballast and the stores plus the men made the lifeboat ride low in the water. Despite the canvas decking, water splashed into the cockpit and the men began to bail before they were out of sight of land.

At first, in the loose ice, there was little wave motion and the men rowed toward the open sea, fending off the floes that swept by in the fast current.

Seated at the tiller, Shackleton searched the ice ahead for leads. He found one running in the direction they wanted to go: north. Until late in the afternoon the men rowed constantly. When one set of oarsmen was spent, another took its place.

They reached the edge of the pack at dusk. It was a mixed blessing. The boat was buffeted by the storm winds from the southwest. The strong sea, unopposed by ice, sent quantities of water over the side. The boat tossed up and down. The motion was so violent that the men had to hold fast to thwarts and gunwales when making their way forward or aft. Spray drenched them all and their woolen clothes became cold, sodden masses. There was no protection from the cold or the wind or the spray.

By nightfall everyone was exhausted. Weakened more than they realized by their past experiences, the men sat listlessly on the thwarts or crept forward beneath the deck to rest on the sleeping bags. The few rough days on Elephant Island had not been enough to heal the frostbitten hands or the sore, split lips.

That first night Shackleton sat at the tiller with Worsley beside him and sent everyone else forward to sleep. Clouds covered the stars. The only visible thing in the darkness was the white crest of the next approaching wave. Worsley managed to light the stove and boil some water. He put in the dried milk and made his way slowly back beside Shackleton with two cups of steaming liquid. Their talk centered on a landfall. South Georgia Island seemed best in plan, but neither man had decided inflexibly on it.

Cape Horn lay to the west — and not so far away as South Georgia. But with a prevailing wind blowing from the Horn, they knew it would be senseless to turn into it and try to work their way west. The Falkland Islands lay due north, but they were farther away than South Georgia. With characteristic speed, Shackleton decided they would head straight north for two days to get away from the ice, then turn east until they raised South Georgia.

With that problem out of the way, Shackleton began telling yarns, quoting lines from Browning, his favorite poet, and reminiscing about other adventures. After an hour of talking he fell silent and Worsley glanced at him to see if he had fallen asleep. But Shackleton was staring off into the darkness, a quizzical look on his face.

"You know, Skipper," he said at last, "we've had some great adventures together but this is the greatest. This time it's really do or die, as they say in storybooks."

Thinking of the trials that lay ahead, Worsley silently agreed with him. Adding up their chances of surviving to rescue the men left behind, Worsley didn't find much comfort. He glanced again at Shackleton and saw the Boss was worrying, too.

"Well," Worsley said as confidently as he could, "if you can't pull through, I don't know who can."

The words banished the frown on Shackleton's face and he grinned. He stuck out his chin, hunched his shoulders and stirred restlessly. "You're right," he agreed enthusiastically. "Of course we'll do it. Look how we've got through everything else."

His optimism restored, Shackleton braced himself against the stern and said, "I wish I'd been able to explore further south though. Still," he added, "we've got two hundred miles of new coast to our credit." He glanced back over his shoulder toward the Antarctic. "When we get back," he said, "if the war's over, we'll have another go at it . . . try to get across the whole continent. What do you say?"

Worsley could think of nothing to say in the face of such optimism. He simply nodded and gulped down the last of his milk.

"Do you think there's gold there?" Shackleton asked abruptly.

Worsley shrugged. "I don't know," he said. "But I found a pearl lagoon once out in the Pacific. When we get back, let's go find it."

Dreaming dreams again, Shackleton agreed without hesitation. The fact that he was being inconsistent didn't bother him. "Right," he said quickly. "No more shivering on ice floes. Palm trees and coral islands after this." Then he added, almost wistfully, "I wonder what we'd have seen though, if we'd gone a few miles inland. Maybe the highest mountain in the world. Maybe a chain of volcanoes. Who knows what else?"

They were well north of the pack ice by now. Waves running free from Cape Horn hundreds of miles away treated the boat as though it were a stick of wood. From crest to trough each wave was higher than a two-story house. At each crest the wind whipped spray across their faces; the sail snapped taut. In each trough the wind died and the sail hung slack. It was in these moments of comparative calm and quiet that they were able to make themselves heard.

"I wonder how the boys are feeling on the island?" Shackleton asked.

Knowing he'd worry day and night about the men left behind, Worsley tried to relieve the anxiety.

"With a little luck, we'll be getting them off in three weeks or so."

"You know, I've always been set against splitting up the party," Shackleton said, still worrying. "At least they're in good hands. Wild will look after them. You know half of them are children. Remember how I had to tell you to look out for Lees? And then he went and got mixed up with that sea leopard."

Worsley laughed at the memory — and Shackleton's paternal concern.

"It's nothing to laugh at," Shackleton said, grunting, as the tiny boat lurched and rose from another trough. Shackleton eyed the next wave and eased the tiller slightly. The wave struck the boat and spray dashed into their faces for the thousandth time. "Foolhardiness," he shouted above the screaming wind, "is the most serious thing in the world."

Worsley grinned. Their present position — precarious, full of danger — would hardly have reassured anyone else that Shackleton felt strongly about foolhardiness. He was remembering the nickname Shackleton had picked up on a previous expedition:

Cautious Jack Shackleton. At the moment it didn't seem appropriate.

When the sky began to lighten, the clouds were seen rushing by overhead. Shackleton eyed them to get the wind direction, smoked and talked on and on and on.

Worsley's head slumped forward and, despite the pitching of the boat, he dozed. They had talked the night through — or at least Shackleton had. Seeing Worsley almost asleep, Shackleton gave him a shove forward to his sleeping bag and called another man to take his place. When the replacement came, dazed, still half asleep, Shackleton pointed to Worsley's vacated spot and went on yarning.

On the second day at sea the southwest wind shifted to north. Unable to beat to windward, the boat was driven south again — toward the ice and away from their goal. Shackleton set a course as close into the wind as possible but still they fell back. The air grew colder as they neared the pack.

Then, as suddenly as it had changed before, the wind veered to the south. A storm sprang up — blowing all the way from the Antarctic continent. The temperature dropped. The men's soaked clothing stiffened as the moisture froze in the fibers. Wind and spray became more painful. But the *James Caird* began to sail north again, running free before the wind.

Shackleton set four-hour watches, one three-man team per watch. One man handled the tiller, another trimmed and set sail while the third bailed out the boat which was shipping more and more water. The canvas decking, secured by the short nails from packing cases, failed to hold. It sagged and began to leak. The men worked a crude pump made of a short length of pipe and a plunger. It required three men to operate it, one to pump, another to hold the pipe steady, while the third kept it pressed firmly against the bottom of the boat. This meant he had his hands submerged in icy water all the time. Anyone who could be spared for a moment bailed with cups and pots. But the bilge never was dry.

Survival became an immense concern. All needed hot food to withstand the cold, wind and water. Preparing it was a Herculean job. Crean, who was cook, would prop the small stove between his feet. Worsley then sat opposite him. Each man braced himself against the wild motion of the sea with his feet pushing against the opposite side of the boat. When a gust of wind died and there was momentary calm,

Crean would strike a match and try to light the stove. If successful, he put the hoosh pot in place and dropped in chips of ice to melt. When that had been accomplished, the sledging ration of beef protein, lard, oatmeal, sugar and salt was crumbled into the water. All the time the ice was melting and the hoosh cooking, Worsley had the job of holding the pot firmly on the stove while Crean held the stove itself. It was like camping on a roller coaster.

At the familiar cry, "Lunch-O!" a ring of cups appeared instantly around the hoosh pot and Crean carefully ladled out the steaming food.

The salt water coming into the boat soon put the men in as pitiable condition as they had been before reaching Elephant Island. Their faces, mouths and hands chafed and cracked. Their knees, scraped raw on rough rock ballast, festered. Salt-water boils appeared. Their legs, tightly encased in socks and finnesko boots, lost all sense of touch. The skin became white and withered. To counteract this "superficial frostbite," as Shackleton called it, Worsley would strip off his boots and socks, soak the socks in the icy water of the ocean, wring them out and put them back on. Oddly, this seemed to warm his legs and feet. Soon all the men adopted the habit — but all were careful lest the waves and current snatch their socks away. There were no extras.

Though the wind was in the south, it was at hurricane force most of the time. The following sea threatened more than once to swamp the boat. Foaming crests would tower over the stern and only at the last minute would the boat rise as the wave slid beneath the keel. While daylight lasted the boat could be steered to keep water from tumbling into it; but, as darkness came and the storm showed no sign of slackening, Shackleton decided to heave to for the night. The men rigged a sea anchor of oars and swung the boat around into the wind. Sail came down. The light boat rode easily over the crests now and the decking over the bow protected it to some extent. With no ice nearby to crush the hull, Shackleton decided not to set watches that night. All hands struggled into their sodden sleeping bags and, huddled together in the bow beneath the canvas deck, they tried to get some sleep.

Everyone was accustomed to the endless motion by now and gradually becoming used to the streams of sea water coming through the leaky deck. Later, the dripping from above seemed to slacken a bit. Half-asleep, the men were only vaguely aware of the change — but it was welcome nonetheless. Then miraculously it stopped altogether, despite the fact that the freezing wind still screamed across the deck. By early morning the men's feet and legs had warmed sufficiently for them to fall completely asleep.

Daylight came but beneath the deck, in darkness, the men slept on. The boat pitched violently up and down as it had been doing all night. But the motion was different. The men stirred uneasily. Shackleton and Worsley woke. They lay in their sleeping bags, neither speaking, as they measured the change in the boat's movements. The other men woke.

"What is it?" one whispered. "What's wrong?"

Wide-awake now, Shackleton got out of his sleeping bag and crawled aft. Worsley followed him.

Mast and rigging and foredeck were sheathed in a heavy cast of ice. With each gust of freezing wind more spray flew over the foundering boat and froze instantly, adding its weight to the ice already formed. The gunwales rode only inches above the sea. One errant wave could fill the boat completely, and if that happened, there'd be no hope of bailing out.

Shackleton called all the men. But before they could reach the cockpit, he'd taken a knife and, slipping forward over the ice sheet, got to the bow where he began to hack desperately at the ice. Ice covered everything and he couldn't get a handhold. He clung to the mast with one arm and chipped at the ice with his free hand. Within moments the icy wind numbed his fingers until he could no longer hold the knife. With the next lurch of the boat he slid back into the cockpit. Worsley moved forward and began to chop. Soon he, too, had to come back. One by one, using knives and spoons, the men took their turns trying to clear the boat. The oars, lashed to the deck, formed a nest where a great hunk of ice had formed. Reluctantly, Shackleton cut the lines and let the sweeping seas carry oars and ice overboard.

During one of Vincent's brief periods of chopping, the sea-anchor line broke. The bow swung immediately away from the wind and the next wave caught the *James Caird* broadside. The roll of the boat was so severe that Vincent began to slide overboard. He clawed at the ice with his fingers to stop himself, but the sheath of frozen water was impenetrable. Water began to pour into the boat over the windward side. Worsley shouted to Vincent to hold on while he lunged forward to try to catch the man's feet. He couldn't reach them. Recklessly, Worsley slid forward across the ice-covered deck and grabbed the mast. Vincent grabbed it too, in the last instant. He clung to it, panting, and stared at the freezing roil of water just below the leeward gunwale. If he slipped, no one could rescue him.

Another wave struck the boat broadside. Worsley pulled himself to his feet and tried to raise sail. His numb fingers fumbled with the ice-coated halyard. When he'd cleared it he raised the sail as fast as he could. It filled with wind and the boat responded to the rudder. One more wave struck the boat's side, and then it was turning so that seas came quartering on the bow. The boat rode more easily.

Cautiously, Worsley and Vincent retreated to the safety of the cockpit. When they reached it they found it half full of water. Everyone fell to work bailing swiftly until the boat rode higher over the crests and responded trimly to the rudder again.

With sail up, Shackleton turned north, running before the gale. But ice still formed. All through that day and the two days that followed the men had to crawl forward, taking their turns at the task of chopping ice. When they weren't bailing or chipping ice, they got hot food and what little sleep they could.

On the morning of the sixth day at sea, the storm blew itself out. The wind shifted until it was quartering from the south. The sun rose in a clear sky. The men, soaked and weary, squinted in the unaccustomed light. The warmth seemed too good to be true. Ice still clinging to the boat soon melted in the sun's rays. By midday there actually were several dry spots on the canvas deck. The canvas hadn't been dry since the boat left Elephant Island — certainly not dry enough to show up white as it did now.

Knowing the sun's appearance would be brief, the men dragged their sleeping bags from beneath the deck and laid them out to dry. But as the welcome warmth evaporated the water from clothing and bags another problem arose. After the months and months of being soaked, the reindeer hair began to fall from the sleeping bags. Soon the hair had penetrated everywhere. It fouled the pump, crept down the men's backs and beneath their clothing where it itched and smarted. It got into tobacco, pockets, eyes, noses and, worst of all, into the food. That day, when Crean cooked up the hoosh, the men looked on in disgust as he reached into the pot and drew out a great gob of reindeer hair. With admirable economy, Crean squeezed out the ball of hair over the pot before throwing it overside.

During their six torturous days at sea, Worsley had estimated their progress solely by dead reckoning — a precarious method of navigating at best. Now, with the sun out, he took his sextant and went to the bow. Wrapping his arm around the mast, he took his sight. When he had finished calculating their position he announced they were a little more than halfway to their goal.

That news was cheering enough but, looking at the men, Shackleton knew their chances of survival still were not good. Vincent and McNeish showed signs of collapsing altogether. Worsley suffered from cramps and several times after taking his turn at the tiller he could not straighten himself. In one instance he had to be kicked in the stomach before the cramped muscles could be made to function. Shackleton himself suffered from sciatica, a painful and crippling ailment of the hip.

McCarthy remained cheerful and Crean went

about his duties with his usual gusto. To the others it seemed that Crean took to physical discomfort with the same satisfaction another man might take to his fireside chair. At the tiller during the long night watches, Crean sang. At least the others thought that was what he was doing. What they heard was a low, monotonous chant; unintelligible and unvarying as the hymn of a tone-deaf monk. During the day, Crean would burst out enthusiastically with "The Wearing of the Green." While the tune was recognizable, it drew no compliments. Undeterred by the lack of appreciation, Crean would revert to his monotone and continue his unfathomable musical entertainment.

The good weather did not last. On the evening of the eighth day, thick, heavy clouds brought darkness earlier than usual. Wind from the southwest freshened. Soon it was hurling the spray from wave crests, sending long trails of spume off into the darkness. It reached hurricane force and the waves grew higher.

Shackleton took the tiller. The others on his watch began bailing. Despite the pain in his hip, Shackleton stayed at the tiller all that night. Seated in the stern sheets, hunched over, soaking wet and beyond shivering from cold, Shackleton dreamed of the warm comforts aboard a regular ship — where, despite outside weather, a sailor could go below for a hot drink and sleep in a warm, dry bunk. He thought of his favorite lines from Coleridge and said them aloud, "Alone, alone, all all alone, Alone on a wide, wide sea."

In the cold and darkness they seemed apt. No one in the world knew where they were. In fact, no one but the men on Elephant Island even suspected that they existed. The sea indeed was wide. And they were alone.

Shackleton spent that night fighting the tiller, the storm, the pain in his body — and continued to recite poetry.

Toward morning he peered toward the eastern horizon hoping to see daylight. But clouds and sea were one impenetrable curtain. Still, he kept looking. As the boat rose on the crest of a wave he'd squint in all directions looking for a break in the clouds that would herald a new and perhaps better day.

Finally, on top of a wave, he saw a long white line stretching from south to north. It could be the light between clouds and sea. The boat sank into a trough and he waited for the next wave. When he rose to the crest he looked again. The line was there all right. Nearer now, and wider.

"It's clearing, boys," he called down to the men.

On the crest of the next wave he saw his mistake. In all his years at sea he had never witnessed anything like it. Stretching away into the distance was the white, foaming crest of a tidal wave. Already the roar of approach was audible beneath the high keening of the wind and crash of nearer waves. It bore down on the *James Caird* with express-train speed.

"Hold on for your lives!" Shackleton shouted as the wave towered above the boat. Then the swelling wave front began to suck them up toward the roaring, maelstrom crest.

ten
THOSE LEFT BEHIND

THE day after the *James Caird* boat party left Elephant Island, the ice pack moved in on the shore. Winter had come.

Frank Wild set the men to work building a hut in which they'd have better hope of surviving the cold and wind than in their worn tents. First, the men dug an ice cave in the glacier. But once it had been dug, the warmth of their bodies melted the ice of walls, ceiling and floor and the deluge drove them out. The work was not altogether wasted for the cave served as a storehouse for food and material that otherwise would have been blown or washed from the beach.

Next, the men dragged stones to a site where they built a foundation. The men were weak; some lay sick, unable to help. Blizzards drove them into tents for days at a time. When the walls were four feet high, Wild ordered the two boats placed, bottoms up, over them to serve as a roof. They were tied firmly in place with lines, and canvas was stretched across the keels. Small stones and dirt partially filled the chinks. Snow, packed against the sides, kept out the wind. A piece of canvas over the doorway completed the crude shelter.

Into an area the size of an average living room — and with only a four-foot ceiling — went twenty-two men and their supplies. In addition to being small, the interior of the hut was as dark as the inside of a closed trunk. Only when someone struck a match to light his pipe could anything be seen. The earth and snow chinking were thorough. There wasn't a ray of light from outside to relieve the blackness. Exasperated, Wild rigged two lamps using sardine cans, medical-gauze wicks and seal oil for fuel. These makeshift lights flickered and smoked — but at least they let the men find their way over or around their companions. Finally Wild cut four portholes in the sides of the hut. He glazed one with the glass from the chronometer case and the remaining three with celluloid from photographic supply boxes. The lamps and portholes solved the problem of light but two other troubles harassed the men.

One was smoke. When they first moved into the hut the cookstove was left outside. But as one storm followed another, it became impossible to go out to cook — so the stove came inside. Sooty smoke from the blubber fuel nearly asphyxiated the men. Some were temporarily blinded. Finally Wild rigged piping made of tins and cut a hole through the "roof" to draw off the greasy smoke.

The second problem was drainage. Whenever the sun shone briefly or the weather warmed a little, water from the melting glacier face trickled beneath the foundations and turned the hut floor into a bog. The men dug a hole in the middle of the floor and began to bail. When, by actual count, they dumped out one hundred and sixty gallons in a single day, Wild became so disgusted he ordered a shallow channel cut under the foundation and down to the sea across the beach. Since the beach was made of little but frozen rock it took several days to finish the trench.

The hut was completed just in time. The winter sun sank toward the horizon and the days became long, freezing, depressing twilights. Blizzards raged for days. During brief intervals of calm, the men moved warily about on the beach. It was caution bred of experience. Gaps high in the cliffs behind the camp acted as funnels for sudden gusts of wind that sprang out of nowhere. One instant not a breath of wind would be stirring on the beach; the next a hundred-mile-an-hour gust would fall on them. Men washing cooking equipment at the water's edge had pots and plates torn from their fingers and flung out to sea. One day, four men were shaking out a piece of a tent when the wind came. It tore the canvas from their grasp and sent it sailing far out on the pack ice.

Men themselves were in danger. While trying to dig up frozen sealmeat buried on the beach one day, Hussey labored with a pick in a dead calm. Suddenly the wind rose. Before he could get to the hut it pushed him, stumbling helplessly, toward the ice and the sea. He called for help. But the wind driving the other way sent his shouts in the wrong direction. He struggled against the wind with all his strength but it wasn't enough. Just before he was pushed onto the sea ice — where he'd have been surely lost — he managed to drive the pick into the beach. He clung to it, waiting for the gust to pass.

Men in the hut saw his predicament but none could rescue him until the wind died. When it did, they rushed out and helped him toward safety.

Being blown into the sea was not the only danger on the beach. A man could be decapitated if he were outside at the wrong moment. When the wind came, eddying, beating in all directions, sheets of ice three feet across and inches thick flew off the glacier and mountain peaks. These chunks — as dangerous as flying plate glass — pinwheeled through the air and crashed on the rocks.

The men spent long hours hunting for food as their reserves dwindled. A few remaining seals sighted on the ice near the shore were carefully stalked and killed to provide meat for food and blubber for fuel. Without fuel to cook with, they could not survive. The only other source of food was penguins — the one or two that had not migrated northward with their fellows. When the men came on one and killed it, they dissected it eagerly to have a look at the contents of the bird's stomach. If they were lucky, they found undigested fish there which were prized as a change from seal and penguin meat.

The hunters' luck could not last. Seals and penguins became rarities. The men began digging up old seal bones and bits of meat they had thrown away during days when food was plentiful. With these bits they made stews. When even that refuse was gone, the men spent hours plunging their arms into pools of icy water near the shore to gather limpets. These tiny shellfish, together with seaweed and ancient seal bones, were cooked into a strange, thin stew.

Darkness and monotony became subtle enemies. Days were only short periods of twilight; nights, long, dark nerve-racking periods when sleep would not come. Inside the hut the flickering light from the lamps somehow made the surrounding darkness more depressing. In that dim light the men sewed their clothes — which were falling apart — and read from the scanty library that had been salvaged. This consisted of two volumes from a set of the *Britannica,* two books of poetry, an account of Nordenskjöld's expedition, and a little cookbook of Marston's. The cookbook was the favorite. The men would lie in the dark recesses of the hut while one under the lamp would read his favorite recipe. Then each one would describe his favorite dinner in great detail.

The greatest lack in the men's diet was carbohydrates and they felt it keenly. They longed for cereals and cursed futilely each time they recalled how, in years at home, they'd refused second helpings of pudding.

Even in the extremity Wild would not touch the emergency rations. A fourteen-day supply of good food lay within reach. But it had to be saved. If by spring they had not been rescued, they would have to try to get to Deception Island. They'd need the rations for that.

As the days passed Blackboro's frostbitten feet became worse. Gangrene appeared on his left foot. Macklin and McIlroy decided that amputation of the toes of the foot was the only way to save his life. They made their decision believing they had no anesthetic. But while rummaging through the supplies, one of them found a bottle containing a little chloroform. It wasn't an adequate supply but it was better than nothing.

Their greatest worry was not the operation itself, but the shock following it. In the intense cold, and under the conditions in which they were living, the young patient could die.

To raise the temperature of the hut — and the patient's chances of living — the men eliminated all possible drafts by packing extra snow around the hut. Then everyone but Blackboro and the doctors stood outside to make room for the operation. By using extra quantities of fuel in the small lamps and lighting the cookstove, they managed to warm the "operating room."

The men waited patiently on the beach. Inside, the doctors worked by the light of the dim, smoky lamps. When they emerged, Blackboro was minus toes but no longer suffering from gangrene. The men wrapped extra blankets around the young man and he was given the best possible care.

Blackboro wasn't the only invalid. Heart strain still bothered some of the men as their privations increased. Reacting in another way to the unrelieved stress, some became irrational for days. Through it all, Wild and the other able men worked to help the sick and restore them to normalcy.

Each Saturday night they drank a ritual toast of medical alcohol, hot water, sugar and ginger powder. Hussey's banjo — scarcely usable — produced music and the men sang their favorite songs.

With the winter ice pack barring the approach of any ship, there was no hope of rescue. Frequently, however, southwest storms broke the pack and swept

the ice away briefly leaving open water near the
shore. On such days Wild called to everyone in the
early morning, "Lash up and stow, boys, the Boss
may be coming back today."

But those days were few. As each one passed
with no sign of a ship, even Wild's hope faded.

eleven
STORM-WRACKED

FAR out at sea, the *James Caird* rose toward the crest of the tidal wave. Eddies spun the boat about. The noise deafened the men. They could do nothing but hang onto gunwales and thwarts.

Then it struck. Foam, mountains high, deluged them. Spray beat at them from all sides. A strange white blindness dimmed their vision. Water poured into the boat from every direction.

After what seemed an incredibly long time, the wave passed. The spinning of the boat slowed; the noise lessened and the *James Caird* wallowed in the trough of the sea, half-filled with water. The Primus stove floated about in the cockpit while sleeping bags bumped against the underside of the canvas deck.

As soon as they recovered from the shock, the

men grabbed cups and began to bail as fast as they could. The *James Caird* had never been nearer foundering. It rolled broadside to the waves, in danger of capsizing at any moment.

When the boat began to respond to the tiller, Shackleton turned the bow into the wind. The exhausted men bailed more slowly as the hours passed. Gradually the water level in the boat went down and the *James Caird* rode high on the water again. Momentarily safe, the men rested on the thwarts. Crean, swearing weakly, tried to light the Primus to prepare hot food and drink. It took three hours.

On the twelfth day at sea Worsley tried to take a sight with the sextant. Since leaving Elephant Island, he'd been able to shoot the sun only four times. According to his estimate they should be near South Georgia. But such navigation could be far wrong.

Shackleton steadied the boat to give Worsley as stable a deck as possible. Despite his efforts the boat pitched and rolled in the heavy sea, going up and down erratically. Worsley braced himself and took a reading. With all odds against accuracy, his shot contained elements of skill, luck and what amounted to mystic intuition. At noon, when he tried to determine his latitude, high fog obscured the sun. So he aimed at the large circle of brightness behind which lay his target. To compensate for error, he took ten readings and averaged them. When he'd finished calculating, Worsley announced they were less than a hundred miles off the western tip of South Georgia.

Shackleton immediately altered course to the east. Praying that Worsley's figures were correct and that they would raise land on their new course, he set the men to work checking the remaining stores. The large block of ice that had supplied fresh water was gone. They'd had to tap one of the wooden casks. Now they discovered the sea water in the remaining keg — the one that had been cracked when they were loading supplies for the voyage.

The salty water had to be used. It was all they had. Under other circumstances no one would have been the worse for it. But in their present condition, the brackish liquid made their thirst more acute. They'd been soaked in sea water for days. Salt all over their bodies searched out every raw and cracked place in their skin and attacked it with all its chemical force. Every time they put their hands to their mouths they carried more salt to lips so swollen that talking was painful. Hands and wrists became inflamed. Sores caused by scraping over the rock ballast festered and grew larger as salt worked into them. Tongues thickened and dried in parched mouths. Movements slowed. Talking stopped.

The morning of May 8th broke thick and stormy. Swells swept them indifferently onward. By midmorning the clouds were so low they seemed to be touching the wave crests. The men sagged listlessly in the boat. Then Worsley raised his arm slowly and pointed ahead. A piece of kelp floated by. Minutes later a larger bit of seaweed came into view. On it sat two "shags," birds that rarely wander more than ten or fifteen miles from shore. Everyone stared eastward for a sight of land, but the mist and clouds hid whatever lay ahead.

A little past noon, McCarthy, who was peering doggedly across the wind-swept water, glanced upward through a break in the clouds. He saw black rock cliffs instead of sky. Then the clouds parted and everyone saw them — as menacing and unapproachable as the cliffs of Elephant Island.

As the boat drew nearer, everyone heard the ominous boom of surf. Then they saw jagged reefs, smothered regularly by white water when the waves struck. Beyond the reefs they saw green tussock grass on ledges high above the sea. Somewhere on that shore streams of fresh water ran wastefully into the sea.

Shackleton sailed as close to the reef as he dared and turned along the coast searching for a gap in the rocks. But they formed an unbroken line as far as he could see.

The light of the short winter day faded. The men stared helplessly through the deepening gloom toward shore.

"Let's take a chance," Worsley mumbled through his swollen lips.

Shackleton shook his head. "In the morning," he said. "We'll land in the morning." He turned the boat toward the sea again, tacking out to make an offing for the long night ahead.

The men scarcely could eat food that night, their mouths and tongues were so swollen. The one water cask held only a pint of dirty brackish liquid. To make it drinkable, the men carefully filtered the water through medical gauze. That got rid of some of the dirt but it still was salty.

All that terrible night the crash of distant surf

filled their ears. They couldn't sleep but sat crumpled in the boat waiting for each moment to pass until daylight came and they could land.

But the sea was not finished with them yet.

Early on the morning of May 9th the wind shifted to the northwest. Within an hour it rose to storm force. Daylight seeped through the low, hurrying clouds, yellow and unpleasant. Gulls fled downwind. Then the hurricane struck.

The sea turned to a froth of white as the screaming wind whipped the surface. It lashed the waves so hard it drove the crests up into the air turning the sky itself into a blinding, opaque sheet.

The boat was on a dead lee shore. Within minutes of the storm's beginning, the sound of the surf was noticeably louder. The hurricane was driving them directly toward the reefs and the tall, black cliffs.

Shackleton ordered the double-reefed mainsail raised in the face of the hurricane. Men manned the two remaining oars. The others bailed constantly.

The boat seemed to be on a rushing treadmill. Seas swept under the keel and crashed a few yards away on the reef. The sail filled with wind and the men rowed, white-faced, in the last extremity of exhaustion. And yet the boat seemed to remain motionless.

The bow, turned into the wind, began to pound the waves that sped by. Each time the keel struck a wave the worn seams opened and water spurted in. The boat quivered from stem to stern.

Shackleton sat grimly holding the tiller, heading the boat close to the wind. Everyone except the oarsmen bailed without looking at the nearby rocks. The thunder of surf was all the warning they needed. Hunger, thirst and weariness were forgotten. At their backs rose the gaunt, rock cliffs of the island they had tried so hard to reach — and now could not touch.

Tacking, rowing, bailing, they struggled for an offing. Their progress was measured in feet. Every few minutes Shackleton glanced at the ugly reef and estimated the distance to it. It seemed to be lengthening a little. But while they were holding their own, perhaps gaining a few feet of safety, a strong current was sweeping the boat along the shore. Looking in the direction it was taking them, Shackleton saw they were heading directly for a small, rocky, offshore island that lay outside the reef. Worsley saw it too. Neither man relaxed his efforts.

The boat inched seaward as the current swept it toward destruction. It was now only a question of the speed of the current versus the speed of their progress offshore.

"She'll make it!" Worsley shouted, still bailing.

"Of course she will!" Shackleton shouted back. "She's damn well got to."

When the *James Caird* came to the outcropping rock, the stern swept by only a few feet from it.

The men moved now like automatons, mechanical dolls that were slowly running down. They bailed; they rowed — dumbly, with mouths hanging open, breath whistling in and out of dry, rasping throats. All that day they worked. They couldn't stop for rest or food.

The storm lasted until darkness. Then the wind shifted. Just as it did, the pin holding the mast worked loose and the sail fell to the deck. The men stared at it. If it had fallen while the storm was at its height, nothing could have saved them from dying on the reef.

Silently, Worsley repaired the mast and raised the tattered sail. When he'd finished, Shackleton turned the boat seaward again. They could not find a way through the reef during the night. Worsley rigged a sea anchor and the boat lay to, waiting once more for daylight.

Water sloshed in the bilge. All the drinking water was gone.

Shackleton didn't expect everyone to survive the night. But when the morning of May 10th came, bright and windless, miraculously, they all were alive.

Huge swells, aftereffects of the storm, slammed into the reef and the cliffs of the island. Each reflected wave met others headed shoreward and a great cross sea was running. Worsley and Crean raised the sail and Shackleton turned the boat eastward along the coast once more in search of a channel through which he could take the boat.

At 8 A.M. the wind shifted to northwest and Worsley looked up anxiously at the low-flying clouds. Another storm was coming.

The wind rose and the boat made its way close to the reef while everyone looked for an opening. They knew they couldn't survive another hurricane.

At noon Shackleton pointed to a large bay behind the reef. Quiet water stretched inland for miles. Then dead ahead he saw a narrow opening in the rocks. Surf boiled on either side of the channel but he knew they had to try it.

When he turned the bow toward the opening in the reef, a strong offshore wind drove them back. Four times Shackleton brought the boat up to the channel. Four times he had to fall off and turn, to come back and try again. On the fifth attempt, sailing close to the wind, he edged through a gap so narrow the oarsmen had to ship oars to keep them from breaking on the rocks.

The boat moved slowly into King Haakon Bay on the southern shore of South Georgia. The bow came to rest on a rocky beach in a little cove. Shackleton jumped out to hold the boat. He grabbed the painter and walked up the beach only to stumble and fall knee deep into a stream of cold, fresh water that ran gurgling across the rocks to the sea.

twelve

TOO-SOLID LAND

THE men crawled over the gunwales and staggered onto the rocky beach. While two of them held the boat, the others buried their faces in the stream of ice-cold water and drank until they could drink no more. Then they went back and gave the others a chance to drink.

There was no exultation in landing, no back-slapping, no great cry of relief. They were too near death for any display of emotion. Vincent and Mc-Neish had to be helped from the boat and almost carried to the fresh water.

The next need was hot food and drink. Crean set up the Primus and boiled milk which the men drank greedily. Then, exploring a little way along the cliff that formed the side of the cove, Crean found a sheltered spot for a camp. Actually, it was a cave in the cliff face. The entrance was hung with great icicles but farther back it widened out and was comparatively dry.

Shackleton ordered supplies, stove and wet sleeping bags dragged into their "home." Crean lit the stove again and began to boil a hoosh. The men holding the boat on the beach struggled hard to pull it out of reach of the surf but they were too weak to drag the *Caird* all the way up. Swells crashed against the stern. Before they could move the boat at all the rudder was torn away and lost in the sea.

At eight o'clock, after a hot meal, Shackleton sent all the men to bed. He went to the beach and stood the first watch guarding the boat. Alone, in the wind and darkness on that rocky shore, he wrestled with the waves, straining first one way and then another to keep the boat from splintering on the shore. As a wave withdrew from the beach, it took the boat with it and he had to pay out the painter slowly lest the force of the wave snap the one remaining rope. At times he even had to plunge into the surf to safeguard the *Caird*.

After five hours' struggle, Shackleton felt his strength going and he called Crean to relieve him. Before Shackleton slept, he organized one-hour watches for the men during the remainder of the night.

In the morning, with a supply of fresh water at their doorstep, the men turned their attention to replenishing their food supply. High on a slope above the cave, Crean, Shackleton, McCarthy and Worsley found an albatross rookery. The nesting birds had hatched out their chicks and the youngsters — each weighing about fourteen pounds — looked good to the hungry men. They took four chicks back with them to camp and that night Crean stewed them, using sledging ration for gravy. With that feast, Worsley's exuberance returned and he fell to scheming with Shackleton about taking albatross chicks to sell to epicures and gourmets in Europe. In his excitement he forgot that the albatross, so much a part of sea lore, is protected by law.

When they had eaten their fill, they rolled cigarettes using scraps of remaining tobacco and lolled back on their sleeping bags to enjoy the luxury of their smoke-filled cave on the desolate shore of South Georgia.

As soon as the first watchman took his place beside the boat that evening, the others fell asleep. It was a fitful, restless sleep. Some men simply leaned against the walls of the cave and dozed. Others struggled into the damp sleeping bags and fell asleep. They muttered and turned to and fro in their exhaustion. During the night Shackleton suddenly sat up, apparently wide awake, and called, "Look out! Look out, boys! And hold on! It'll get us!"

Worsley struggled upright and asked, "What is it?"

"Look at that big sea breaking!" Shackleton pointed out the cave opening.

Worsley stared outside but saw only the snow-topped black cliffs across the Sound.

When Shackleton had been fully roused from his nightmare of the tidal wave, he lay down once more and tried to sleep.

In the early morning hours the watchman on duty called out, waking the men to a more material danger. Everyone rushed to help and found Crean struggling in water up to his waist, holding the *James Caird* by the painter that had come untied from the boulder on shore. The sea was dragging both Crean and boat away. The men plunged into the ice-cold water and managed to pull the boat partially up on the land. But the current still gripped it.

The rest of that night the men clung to the boat,

half-frozen, weak, their spirits reduced nearly to zero. At the worst moment, when it seemed none could hang on much longer, Shackleton spoke in the darkness. "I hope," he said with grave formality, "you're all enjoying my little party."

When daylight and low tide came, the men managed to secure the boat. Frostbitten and weary, they stood on the shore and looked gloomily about them. Ice blocked the entrance to the cove in which they'd taken shelter. They were trapped.

For three days they lived in the cave waiting for the ice to go out. On the fourth, the morning light showed open water to the main channel of the Sound. Shackleton hastily ordered the boat launched. Crean and McNeish worked to rig an oar as a rudder while the rest of the men loaded supplies. Then Crean spotted an object floating in on the swells. He gave a shout and scrambled for it. The lost rudder had been returned miraculously, by tides and currents, to the very spot from which it had been taken. Gleefully Crean tossed it into the boat and climbed aboard. With sail set, the *James Caird* moved slowly up the Sound toward a better camping place.

Shackleton kept to the main channel and avoided

small inlets and coves where ice could paralyze further movement. Rounding a point of land, they sighted a high, grassy slope above a shelving beach. Beyond that lay a rocky point on which was a great herd of sea elephants. Shackleton landed immediately. The men hauled the boat up well out of the water. They had found what they were looking for: a safe camp site plus an unlimited supply of fresh meat and fuel.

At this landing place they stripped the *James Caird* completely. Even the raised sides McNeish had built on the ice of the Weddell Sea so many months ago were torn off. They overturned the boat, packed sod around the openings and stowed the sleeping bags inside. Peggoty Camp was established. In the late afternoon the smell of broiling sea-elephant steak filled the air. The blubber, burned as fuel, sent a column of thick, sooty smoke high above the camp.

Rested and fed, Shackleton and Worsley discussed the next move. By sea, the distance to the whaling stations on the other side of the island was over 150 miles. In the winter storms they would surely encounter, the boat could be swept far away from the stations. In any case, a thorough examination of the *James Caird* showed it would never be seaworthy again. The pounding seas, the battering ice, had reduced it to a near wreck.

The only alternative was to walk across the island.

Next morning Worsley and Shackleton began scouting the land farther up the Sound for a possible route to the interior. Tramping around a large point of rock, they came upon a sight that stopped them in their tracks.

In the cove beyond the point lay half an acre of beached flotsam from the sea. Here were pieces of oars, masts, planking, prows, spars, deck rails, cabin housings, hatchcovers — everything that might float from a wreck. They saw pieces of wood with ancient figureheads carved on them, teakwood stanchions, iron-strapped beams with the iron nearly rusted through. It was a graveyard of ships that had foundered in storms off the legendary Cape Horn.

It seemed, as they looked at the great pile of sea wrack, that they had come upon a sight not meant for human eyes. For a moment their own predicament was forgotten as the sight evoked a thousand tragedies, nameless and now forgotten.

Worsley stooped and picked up a bit of wood.

It was a child's boat — stripped of paint, nearly formless, yet still recognizable. Shackleton and Worsley looked at it in silence. Worsley tossed it down on the rocks where it clattered and lay still. Both men walked farther along the beach away from that depressing sight.

On the following days, Worsley and Shackleton tramped miles of coastline, climbing the rocky slopes, peering upward across glaciers and snowfields to find a pathway to lead them over the mountains of South Georgia.

They knew the trip would not be easy. Everyone who had ever looked at the bleak mountains or suffered through storms that howled down from the interior glaciers agreed: no human being who tried to cross South Georgia could live.

thirteen
BEYOND ENDURANCE

THE long dimension of South Georgia Island runs approximately northwest to southeast. Along its back is the Allardyce Mountain range which rises over 9000 feet above the sea. At right angles to this string of mountains, like ribs sprouting from a backbone, are lesser ranges. In reality they are giant hurdles to be overcome by any traveler from King Haakon Bay to Stromness Bay. Between all the glittering, rocky peaks of the mountains lies a sheet of ice hundreds of feet thick and covered in places by vast snow-fields. In the gaps between the mountains, running down off the high inland plateau, glaciers grind their way slowly to the sea.

The few beaches along the coast rapidly give way to rocky slopes leading to the plateau, or to unscalable cliffs. No whaleman, visitor or explorer had ever penetrated more than a mile from the sea anywhere on its coast and, except for the whaling stations grouped on the shores of Stromness Bay, no human settlement had existed on the island.

Shackleton's plan was to leave the sick men, Vincent and McNeish, in the care of the ever-cheerful McCarthy while he, Worsley and Crean set out on the journey. These three men proposed to cross the unmapped interior of South Georgia during wintertime. None had experience in mountain climbing. They had no equipment that experienced mountaineers regard as essential. In fact, they had no real choice of any equipment. Losses and abandonment of material had reduced their supplies to food, a little fuel oil, a Primus stove and hoosh pot, one pair of binoculars, a fifty-foot length of rope, a small hand compass, a chronometer, and a carpenter's adze that Shackleton thought might prove useful to chop steps in the ice.

King Haakon Bay lies about a third of the way down the southern coast of the island. The whaling stations are at the northeast end. The distance, as the crow flies, is a little over eighteen miles. But the men's route would wind up through the first snow slopes, onto the plateau where the ice sheet spread around the mountain peaks. They would have to skirt crevasses, find pathways through unexplored land, fight storms and constant below-freezing temperatures. No one knew what distance they would have to cover. It might be twenty, forty or a hundred miles of rock and ice and snow. But distance was not the main problem. The nature of the land itself and time loomed larger in their minds. They could take neither tent nor sleeping bags — and that meant they would have to make the trip in one long, sustained dash. They had fuel oil sufficient to cook six meals — beyond that they would either starve or freeze to death if they had not reached Stromness. They could never turn back.

While Crean, Worsley and Shackleton collected and repaired their gear, McNeish drew brass screws from the hull of the boat and fastened them to the soles of the travelers' boots — the only concession they could make to the ice cliffs that lay ahead.

On the night of May 18, 1916, Shackleton and his men slept under the shelter of the upturned boat for the last time. At one o'clock on the morning of May 19th, after very little actual sleep, they rose, cooked a hot meal and began to load themselves with their meager equipment.

The full moon shone brightly on the little party as the men struggled with items to be carried. Worsley slung the chronometer and binoculars around his neck — and tucked a pair of semidry socks beneath the straps back of his neck to ease the strain. Shackleton carried the adze and rope, Crean the stove and hoosh pot with their meals stowed in it.

They said good-by to Vincent, McCarthy and McNeish. McNeish walked with them along the rocky shore toward the steep slope up which they would go. But after going two hundred yards, he turned back, exhausted. The final salute of waving hands came from McCarthy and Vincent. Crean, Worsley and Shackleton waved once more, then turned their faces toward the mountains and began to climb.

The snow on the lower slopes was soft. The men sank into it, struggling upward, sweating in the bright moonlight. At the end of two hours they found themselves 2500 feet above sea level. Here, lower temperatures hardened the snow and they walked swiftly across the crust without breaking through. With each step they peered about them to see — for the first time since the world was formed — what the interior of South Georgia Island was like. But sea fog, coming up behind them, obscured their view.

In a few moments the fog wrapped them in a white shroud so thick they couldn't see more than a step ahead. They had to move slowly. They walked close together, almost in a line abreast.

Suddenly Shackleton stopped. A fraction of a second later — before he could call out — Crean and Worsley stopped, too. They were standing on the lip of a chasm, an abyss so deep and so dark they could see nothing in its depths. For a moment no one spoke. One step more, by any of them, would have been his last.

Shackleton had the men rope together and walk farther apart so that if one of them fell into such a chasm, the others could haul him out. Silently, and with hands trembling slightly from their escape from immediate death, the three men lashed the rope around their waists.

Shackleton struck out again, leading the party. He skirted the chasm and started east across the rising slope of ice. The fog was so thick he could not see where he was going. Worsley, bringing up the rear, took out his small pocket compass and glanced at it every step or two to check their course. From time to time the mountain stillness was broken by his voice calling "starboard" or "port" or "steady."

And so three sailors, turned mountaineers, went on their way.

The morning sun came up over the mountains to the east. In its warmth the fog thinned and streamed upward from the snow surface to vanish in the blue sky. Through holes in the fog Shackleton saw the shining surface of a lake ahead. They hurried forward, curious and anxious at the same time. Then the fog disappeared and showed them their mistake. Their "lake" stretched to the horizon. It was an arm of the sea down below the plateau, reaching far inland, blocking their eastward path.

An hour passed before they backtracked enough to get around the bay. Sun on the surface of the snow melted the crust and the men broke through time after time. When they had regained their course, Shackleton ordered a halt to cook their first meal.

To protect the stove from the constant wind, Crean dug a three-foot hole in the snow and lowered the stove into it. Then, carefully, he lit it while Shackleton and Worsley lay full length in the slush to windward of the "kitchen" for added protection.

They all peered anxiously at the hoosh, waiting impatiently for it to boil. Seated in a circle with the pot at the center, the three men began to eat. They had no plates or cups — only a spoon apiece. They took turns dipping their spoons in the hoosh to be sure all got equal portions. After a few rounds of mouthfuls Shackleton looked at Crean and said in an angry voice, "You've got a bigger spoon than either of us."

Crean munched his hoosh contentedly, without flicking an eye. "It doesn't make any difference," he said, taking up the joke. "The Skipper's got a bigger mouth."

Their new course now lay a little south of east to avoid any more "lakes" filled with sea water. Directly ahead in the bright sunlight a range of mountains rose, blocking their path. The peaks, sheer rock spines thrust up through the ice sheet, towered above them. Somehow they had to find a way between them.

For three hours they struggled up the slope toward the range. It gradually steepened and became pure ice with no snow covering at all. Shackleton chopped footholds with his carpenter's adze and they moved step by laborious step toward the pass between the first two peaks. The rim was as sharp as the ridge of a house roof. No one knew what lay on the other side. When they reached the top of the slope all peered over the edge expectantly.

No one spoke. No one had to. Beyond the rim was a sheer cliff of ice plunging 1500 feet down to a mass of sharp jagged chunks of ice that had broken off and fallen, shattering at the foot.

The rim and the mountain range ran north and south. The three men were between two of several peaks that were almost in line. Looking to his right Shackleton saw only high mountains — higher than those of the range they were blocked by. To his left he could see only as far as the next rocky peak. Between them and that peak was the ice rim and the cliff on its eastern face. There was only one possible course to follow: backtrack and go around the peak to the left and hope the ice cliff didn't exist beyond it.

It had taken the men three hours to climb the slope to their high and windy cul-de-sac. It took only an hour to slide down. They cleared the lower part of the mountain, walked around it, and began once more to climb the ever-steepening slope toward the next possible pass.

When they reached the sharp razorback rim of ice again at the top of the slope they looked over. The ice cliff here fell away even more steeply, if possible, and the distance down seemed greater.

They retreated again, rounded another peak and climbed once more to the top. Another cliff blocked their way. Tired and discouraged, they started back down the ice to round yet a third peak.

The short winter day was nearing an end. The wind increased. The temperature dropped. Going north around the third peak they came upon a great canyon in the ice blocking their way. Lying on their stomachs they looked over the edge straight down a thousand feet into a valley of blue ice. It was a bergschrund, or long deep ravine that hurricane winds blowing for untold centuries had carved in the ice sheet.

There was no way to get around the mountains. The ice cliff between the peaks blocked them on the east, the bergschrund on the north, and higher mountains on the south.

Silently, Shackleton, Worsley and Crean drew back from the edge of the bergschrund and walked southeast toward the ice cliff between the nearest two peaks. They stopped once for another meal, protecting the stove from the wind with their bodies again, dipping their spoons one at a time into the hoosh. They ate silently, without benefit of a joke.

When they were finished, Crean shouldered the

stove and hoosh pot, Worsley slung chronometer and binoculars once more around his neck, Shackleton picked up the adze, and they headed up the last slope toward the cliff of ice that waited for them.

Near the rim, ice made a difficult footing. Shackleton swung the adze, chipping steps, moving up one at a time toward the summit from which they could not retreat.

Darkness was on them when they reached the top. The summit of ice was so sharp the three men sat astride it one leg on one side, one on the other.

Wind, blowing hard and cold, penetrated their thin clothing. Looking back down the slope up which they'd struggled, Shackleton saw gray wisps of fog streaming across the snow toward them. He began chopping footholds in the cliff face. Gradually he worked his way down a few feet. When he'd chopped several steps he cleared away enough ice to form a spot where all three could stand at once.

The rising wind whined across the ice rim over their heads. Doggedly Shackleton chopped more steps in the face of the steeply sloping cliff. When he'd worked to the length of the rope, he cleared another platform and Worsley and Crean moved cautiously down beside him.

While waiting for them, Shackleton sat down and stared off into the distance thoughtfully. Neither Worsley nor Crean spoke. Shackleton shivered uncontrollably in the cold wind.

"We'll freeze to death on this cliff," he said.

No one disagreed.

"I've got an idea," Shackleton said after a pause.

Crean and Worsley waited.

"We've got to go on," Shackleton continued, "no matter what's below. This way is hopeless. We can't cut steps down thousands of feet."

Crean and Worsley agreed.

Shackleton sighed. "It's a devil of a risk but we've got to take it. We'll slide."

For a moment even the danger-loving Worsley was speechless. He peered down the cliff but couldn't see bottom. It was hidden in shadows. The cliff itself was as nearly vertical as a church steeple. There might be rocks, ice fragments, anything below.

"All right," he said at last.

Crean leaned over and looked down, too. He couldn't see beyond the line of shadows either and counted it something of a blessing.

Silently the three men untied the fifty-foot length of rope from their waists and coiled it. Shackleton sat on the forward end, Worsley in the middle and Crean on the rear. They grabbed each other around the waist, toboggan-fashion, locked feet around legs and, without another word, Shackleton kicked them off into space.

For an instant they seemed to hang motionless in the darkening air — then they shot down the cliff. At the first sensation of near-falling, Worsley's voice froze in his throat. No one could do anything but hang on with all his strength.

As their speed increased and the wind whistled around their ears a sense of exhilaration came over them all. Worsley shouted with excitement. Crean and Shackleton shouted, too.

One minute passed. They were still intact though in the shadows now and could see nothing.

Two minutes. Their speed increased. If there had been light they couldn't have seen a thing. The landscape was passing in a blur. But they went on shouting.

Three minutes. Their speed lessened. The slope flattened out. In a moment they came to a stop in a bank of snow and fell gasping into the drift.

Laughing, weak with excitement and astonishment, they untangled themselves and began shaking the snow from heads and ears and clothing. Then, standing, miraculously safe, at the foot of the three-thousand-foot cliff, they all solemnly shook hands. "You know," Shackleton said, "it's not good to do that kind of thing too often."

No one agreed more heartily than Worsley who still was brushing snow from his clothes. He leaned over to get the last of it off his boot tops and Shackleton burst out laughing.

"What's the matter?" Worsley straightened up.

"You've torn the seat out of your trousers," Shackleton said.

Worsley inspected his pants angrily. What Shackleton had said was sadly true. And they were his dress trousers at that — the ones salvaged long ago from the hold of the *Endurance*.

Shackleton turned away, still laughing, and then it was Worsley's turn. He pointed to Shackleton's pants which were torn as badly as his.

Crean felt the rear of his own trousers and swore mightily.

Thankful, weary, elated and with chilled rear ends, the three men began to walk eastward again across the snow.

Their course took them once more up a gently rising snow slope. Though darkness had come, they knew they were headed toward another transverse mountain range. Progress was slow in the darkness but at eight o'clock the moon rose, bright and full, lighting their path.

Four hours later they were at an altitude of 4000 feet. Mountains ahead cast dark shadows on the moonlit snow. In the hope of avoiding other ice cliffs Shackleton changed course toward what looked like an easy pass north of the range. But soon the smooth snow surface gave way to a rough, icy one. In a few more hours they were struggling vainly to pass over the dangerous crevasses of a glacier. But large folds of ice and open chasms slowed them until they had to stop. The way that had appeared easy was a trap. They had to turn back and face the mountains again.

As they retraced their steps, they moved more slowly than before. Their strength was going fast. Shackleton ordered stops every ten minutes so each might rest a moment and catch his breath. For twenty-four hours they had been marching across ice and snow in freezing winter temperatures.

Realizing that they were nearing total exhaustion, Shackleton led them to a partially protected nook in the rocks at the bottom of a small slope. The men dumped their equipment on the snow, burrowed down into the drifts to escape the wind. Crean and Worsley fell asleep instantly.

Shackleton's head nodded forward. His plan was to sleep for an hour or so and then continue on their way. But from somewhere deep inside his mind a warning sounded. The quickness with which both Crean and Worsley had fallen asleep startled him. And even in his own weariness, the will to survive made itself felt. Sleep, now, for all of them would be the end. He sensed it and struggled to keep his eyes open. When five minutes had passed, he roused the others. He told them they'd slept for half an hour. Worsley and Crean were so dazed that neither understood Shackleton's necessary deception. Without complaint, they rose and shouldered their equipment. When they started to walk once more their knees were so stiff from cold they moved bent over, like old men.

The waning moon shone on the three figures, black specks on the vast snowfield, making their way toward more mountains. They trudged between two peaks and reached the top of the pass. No one was surprised to find the upward slope ending in a ridge — with an ice cliff on the other side.

The wind had died and their breath hung visible in the freezing air. Silently Shackleton began chopping steps in the cliff face, working his way down the slope. The cliff itself was not so high as the one down which they'd tobogganed but it was even more steep — a sheer, vertical sheet of ice five hundred feet straight down.

Slowly Shackleton worked his way downward, the other two men following. The chip, chip, chip of the adze was the only sound breaking the stillness. Hours passed. The moon set. Darkness was complete.

Shackleton stopped chopping for a moment and peered toward the bottom. Frustrated by their slow progress and the impossibility of finding any other way, he kicked at the cliff face with his heel. To his surprise his foot broke through a crusty layer and he found he'd formed a step with no laborious chopping at all. He tried with his other foot. Again it worked. The east face of the cliff, alternately warmed and frozen by the coming and going of the sun, plastered with layers of snow from countless blizzards, was a penetrable curtain of ice.

Shackleton began to "walk" down the cliff face kicking steps with his heels. Worsley and Crean followed. Their backs were pressed flat against the ice.

Their heads were held firmly against the smooth cliff. Slowly, but with growing excitement, the men continued their descent. One gust of wind from any direction would have blown them off the cliff to death below. But no wind came.

At last they stepped away from the cliff to the snow slope at the bottom and, without pausing to congratulate themselves, hurried eastward. The expanse of snow underfoot was smooth now. Stumbling with weariness, they wandered out on the thinly frozen surface of a lake. Their first awareness of danger came when Crean broke through the ice and plunged into the water. Shackleton and Worsley hauled him out and they got off the lake ice as fast as they could. When they were on safe snow again Shackleton stopped the party and they cooked a hot meal.

In the early morning stillness they heard a steam whistle. For a moment no one spoke. They looked at each other in astonishment. It was the first sound of civilization to reach their ears.

Seven more miles lay between them and the whaling station. But the whistle, calling the men to work, made it seem that they already were there.

As the sun rose, they saw, far below on the shores of the island, the harbor, whaling ships, buildings that meant safety and rest and — most important — rescue for the men on Elephant Island.

Abandoning cooker and stove, the three men hurried across the snow, floundering in the soft deep drifts. Shackleton chose a ravine that led down off the final slope. Almost merrily the three walked along the bottom, their feet sloshing in a stream of melted glacier water. After a few minutes they became aware of a strange roaring sound that made talk or other sounds inaudible.

A thirty-foot waterfall blocked their path. On either side of the falls ice-sheathed rocks rose straight up.

Shackleton quickly chose the only path open to them. "Looks like we'll have to go down in the water, boys," he said.

Worsley uncoiled the rope without protest and looked for some rock around which to tie it. There was none small enough near the top of the falls to serve. Improvising, Worsley laid the end of the line across the top of a large rock in the stream directly above the falls and pounded it into crevices, counting on friction to hold their weights as they tried to slide down.

Crean went first while Shackleton and Worsley

held the rope as best they could. Crean's lanky, raw-boned figure disappeared in the icy water. Then he appeared, soaked to the skin, sputtering and gasping at the bottom. Shackleton worked his way down next in the ice-cold deluge. Worsley, lightest of the three, went last. He didn't expect the rope to hold so he went down sailor fashion, nearly falling as he let the rope slide through his hands until he was about to strike rocks below. Then he grabbed the rope firmly to break his descent. It held firm and all three men stood in the pool at the foot of the last obstacle.

Worsley tried to recover the rope but it had become so firmly wedged in the cracks of the rock he couldn't free it. Not wanting to waste more time, they walked down the stream to the last snow slope, leaving the rope twirling and twisting in the falling water behind them.

Free of the mountains and ice cliffs at last, Shackleton, Worsley and Crean stumbled toward the whaling station. Smoke poured from the factory chimney. They saw men walking about on the shore. Suddenly it occurred to them they were not very presentable. They paused and Worsley produced several rusty safety pins from his pocket. With these they repaired the more embarrassing rips in their clothing.

When they straightened and inspected each other, they grinned. Worsley tried to run his fingers through his hair in a last effort at neatness. But his fingers couldn't penetrate the tangled mass.

They strode toward the nearest building. Two small boys, sons of whalemen, saw them as they approached. The youngsters took one look at Shackleton, Worsley and Crean — then turned without a word and ran away as fast as their legs could carry them.

fourteen
STRANGE WELCOME

STATION manager Sorlle, Shackleton's old friend, was in his house that bright morning of May 20, 1916. The day was remarkably calm for that season of the year. There was only a little wind; the sun warmed the beach and the buildings. A few wisps of clouds sailed overhead in the blue sky.

A Norwegian whaleship, *The Southern Sky*, lay at anchor. Men swarmed over the decks and down into the holds. They were busy dismantling the engine and storing parts of it, closing up the ship tight for the worst winter months that lay ahead. *The Orwell*, another whaleship, lay to in the quiet harbor.

Men went back and forth on the beach carrying out their duties. No one so much as glanced at the great, snow-capped peaks of the mountains and cliffs that formed the interior of the island. They always were hugely, impassably there.

Mr. Sorlle bent over some work at his desk. A whaleman stood beside him. Neither moved when a knock sounded on the door. Mr. Sorlle called "Come in!" and went on with his work.

A workman came in. He closed the door quickly behind him. Then he took off his cap and stood silently waiting.

"Well?" Mr. Sorlle asked, looking up impatiently. The whaleman standing by the manager looked at the workman, too.

The man didn't answer Mr. Sorlle at once. He stood slapping his cap against his leg nervously. He looked frightened.

"There's three funny-looking men outside," he said at last. "They says they walked across the island. They says they know you."

Knowing such a thing was impossible, Mr. Sorlle looked sharply at the man.

"What?" he asked, puzzled.

The man gestured at the closed door with his cap. "I left 'em outside," he added.

Mr. Sorlle got up and, followed by the whaleman, went to the door. He opened it and looked out.

Three men stood there. Their hair and beards were tangled mats of filth and grease. Their faces were black. Jackets and trousers hung in rags. Their boots were nearly worn through. They seemed scarcely able to stand up.

For a long moment no one spoke.

At last Mr. Sorlle found his voice. "Who the hell are you?" he asked, trying to overcome his fright and alarm at the strange sight.

The man in the center asked, "Don't you know me?"

Mr. Sorlle peered more closely at him. "I know your voice," he said doubtfully.

The man smiled a little sadly. "My name is Shackleton," he said.

EPILOGUE

YEARS later, the whaleman who was standing beside Mr. Sorlle that morning said, "Everybody knew Jack Shackleton well and we very sorry he is lost in the ice with all hands. But we not know three terrible-looking bearded men who walk into office off the mountainside that morning . . . Me — I turn away and weep. I think manager weep, too."

As soon as Shackleton spoke his name, Mr. Sorlle realized what had happened. So Worsley and Crean and Cautious Jack Shackleton got the food and baths they had been without for so long. Even then, Shackleton could not rest. The friendly Norwegian whalemen offered a ship and Worsley went to King Haakon Bay to rescue McCarthy, Vincent and McNeish.

Worsley had shaved and gotten new clothes. None

of the three men recognized him when he stepped ashore at Peggoty Camp and they asked, in hurt bewildered tones, why one of their comrades hadn't come to rescue them.

The *James Caird* was brought back too. Word of Shackleton's survival spread to all men on South Georgia and they congregated on the shore to welcome the men from Peggoty Camp. All work on the island stopped. Grizzled Norwegian sailors vied with each other to help haul the *James Caird* up on the beach. Better than any other men in the world, those sailors knew the extent of Shackleton's exploit of sailing more than eight hundred miles across winter seas in a small lifeboat.

On their second evening of civilization Shackleton and his men were treated to a dinner aboard a whaleship. As they entered the cabin where the feast was laid out, all the Norwegian whalemen rose in respectful silence. One ship's captain, a veteran of forty years' whaling experience, stood up to make a short impromptu speech. He spoke in Norwegian — and Mr. Sorlle translated — describing what Shackleton had done. When he finished, the captain pointed to Shackleton and his comrades and announced in a loud voice, "These are *men*."

It is not easy to impress whalemen of the Southern Ocean.

Anxiety for the safety of his men on Elephant Island drove Shackleton to action the next day. He went to the Falkland Islands and finally to the ports of South America in search of ships. Three times he set sail — only to be driven back by ice. Late in August he asked the Chilean government for the use of a small, steel-hulled steamer, the *Yelcho,* to make a fourth attempt. He promised not to take the unprotected ship into the ice and with that assurance the Chilean government granted his request.

When the *Yelcho* neared Elephant Island the ice pack lay only a little way offshore. The *Yelcho*'s captain worked the small steamer carefully through the narrow stretch of open water that might close at any minute. They neared the part of the coast where they'd left the men. Worsley and Shackleton stood in the bow of the *Yelcho* straining to catch a glimpse of survivors.

"There they are!" Worsley yelled suddenly, pointing to the shore.

The *Yelcho*'s engines stopped. A boat was lowered away. Shackleton scrambled excitedly into it and oarsmen pulled toward the beach.

The men on shore danced and waved as they saw the rescue boat approaching. Wild had set fire to the last tin of kerosene to attract the ship's attention. He ordered two of the men to carry Blackboro to a high ledge of rock for a grandstand seat at the rescue.

When the boat neared the beach Shackleton made a megaphone of his hands and called, "Are you all well?"

Frank Wild's bearded, grimy face split in a grin as he heard the Boss's voice across the water.

"All well! All safe, Boss!" he called.

Within an hour everyone was safe aboard the *Yelcho*. The little ship steamed as rapidly as possible northward, away from the treacherous ice.

Not one man who had set sail in the *Endurance* so many months ago had been lost. Though they needed rest and food and care, all were essentially sound. So they went back to civilization — back to home, to England, and to war.

J
919.9
B
BIXBY
THE IMPOSSIBLE JOURNEY OF SIR
ERNEST SHACKLETON

4717

Date Due

FEB 7 '64	DEC 31 '77		
FEB 2 6 '64	R 15 '87		
MAR 2 4 '64	MAR 12 '92		
APR 8 '65	APR 9 '92		
JUN 7 '65	SEP 3 0 2004		
MAR 1 0 '66			
NOV 22 '66			
FEB 22 '80			
Mar 7			
AUG 12 '78			
NOV 29 '77